THE NEW

HACIENDA

THE NEW
HACIENDA

Karen Witynski

Joe P. Carr

Photographs by W. Scott Mitchell

Gibbs Smith, Publisher
Salt Lake City

To my mother, Judith M. Simpson, and the memory of my late father, Stanley S. Witynski. —K.W.
To my father Joe P. Carr Sr., and the memory of my late mother, Ellen Mae Carr. —J.C.

07 06 05   5 4 3 2

Text copyright © 1999 by Karen Witynski and Joe P. Carr
Watercolor illustrations copyright © 1999 by Julie Marshall
Photograph copyrights as noted on page 159

Published by
Gibbs Smith, Publisher
P.O. Box 667
Layton, UT 84041
Orders: (1-800) 748-5439
Visit our Website at www.gibbs-smith.com

Edited by Gail Yngve
Designed by Christine Nasser

Printed and bound in Hong Kong

Library of Congress Cataloging-in-Publication Data

Witynski, Karen, 1960–

   The new hacienda / Karen Witynski and Joe P. Carr; foreword by Eugen Logan Wagner.
  —1st ed.

     p. cm.

    ISBN 0–87905–909–5; 1–58685–261–2 pbk.

    1. Haciendas—Mexico—History. 2. Vernacular architecture—Mexico.
3. Interior decoration—Mexico. I. Carr, Joe P., 1942– . II. Title.
NA8210.M48W57 1999
728.8'0972—DC21   99–25674
                 CIP

Cover: This hacienda still life includes a colonial trunk, antique candelabra, and spurs. Photograph by James Ray Spahn.

Half-Title page: Hacienda Temozón's pool is a magnificent stretch of blue, topped off with stark columns for contemporary interest. Photograph by W. Scott Mitchell.

Title page: Hand-carved stone canales, or water spouts, align a red wall to make a splashy display at Hacienda Temozón. Photograph by W. Scott Mitchell.

Table of Contents: An eighteenth-century colonial sabino table holds a collection of devotional art objects, chalices, santos, and jewelry. Collection of Fred Pottinger. Photograph by James Ray Spahn.

Back Cover: Hacienda Xixim's impressive stairwell leads to a carved-stone shell. Photograph by W. Scott Mitchell.

ACKNOWLEDGMENTS

Many people contributed to this book, sharing their talent and generosity of spirit. First, we wish to express our appreciation to the individuals who were an integral part of shaping this project, including our agent, Betsy Amster, for her fine expertise and friendship; our publisher, Gibbs Smith, for his continued support and pioneering spirit; our editor, Gail Yngve, for her vision and dedication; and our art director, Christine Nasser, for her inspiring artistry and magical talent for combining visuals and words. A heartfelt thanks to Amy Witynski Holmes for her valuable editing assistance; without her help, talent, and encouragement, this book would have never found a finish.

In addition, we are particularly grateful to Eugen Logan Wagner for writing the foreword and generously sharing his extensive knowledge of Mexico. His sound advice and enthusiasm in shaping this book was invaluable. We also extend our gratitude to research assistant Sean Hale who was a valuable part of the project from concept to completion. In addition to his research talents, he served as a liaison during the production of our photo shoots in Mexico. J. Armando Garza also assisted with research and gave generously of his time and knowledge of Mexico.

A special mention of gratitude to the following people who have inspired us with their pioneering vision: Roberto Hernández, Rodolfo Morales, Francisco Toledo, Arq. Esteban San Juan Maldonado, and Paul Alexander Bartlett who documented the beauty of Mexican haciendas for over forty years of his life. Our deep appreciation to Steven J. Bartlett for his permission to reprint his father's illustrations and to Mariana Yampolsky for her kindness in allowing us to reprint her magnificent photographs. Additional thanks to Julie Marshall for her beautiful illustrations.

Many people throughout Mexico went far beyond the call of duty in aiding us. These include Oscar Holm Quiroz, Secretary of Touristic Development of the State of Oaxaca, and Georgina Mungaray Cruz Ahedo, Apolinar Germiniano Luis, Roberto Jiménez Fuentes, and Elizabeth Ricardez Weber. Rosario Maza of the Oaxaca Film Commission also shared many valuable insights. Additionally, the Yucatán Tourism Office called our attention to numerous hacienda projects. Our sincere thanks to Ricardo Dajer Nahum, Secretary of Industrial and Commerce Development, Government of Yucatán, and Ana H. Argarez who was especially dedicated to our photography efforts. Additional thanks to Lic. Cándida Fernádez de Calderón and Lilia Delgado of Fomento Cultural Banamex, A.C., for their gracious assistance. A special thank you to Lic. Manuel Angel Nuñez Soto, Governor of the State of Hidalgo.

A very special group of homeowners let us spend hours, in some cases days, in their homes, photographing interiors. They are credited elsewhere in this book, but we wanted to express a special thanks to Bob Gow, Alejandro and Pilar Patrón, Fred Pottinger, Christopher Holder and Wiggie Andrews, Paul Fullerton and Josefina Larrain, Jorge Fenton, Juan Fenton, Alejandro de la Peña, Ruth McMurtry, Luis Zárate, Sergio Hernández, Dr. and Mrs. D. J. Sibley and the Méndez León Jiménez family. A very special acknowledgement to Hotel Casa del Balam, Mérida, for providing us with a peaceful and beautiful retreat while we were on location in the Yucatán. Additional thanks to the owners and staff of Hacienda Temozón, Hacienda Chichén, and Hacienda Katanchel.

Additionally, the following people helped open doors to locations and experiences we will always cherish: Alberto Valenzuela Hernández, Paola Ramos Espinoza, Arq. Ma. Claudina López Morales, Ann Dibble, Domingo Hernández S., Victor Velasco, Rene Cabrera, Juan Ruiz Padilla, Federico Zarilla, Emilio Martinez Hernández, Israel Olivera Lucas, Lorenzo Ruíz Olivera, Felix Rogelio López, Gino Laurenzo, Anabel Delgado, Rosario Marin, Benigno A. Diaz Martinez, and Miguel F. Faller Cervera. Our sincere gratitude to Juan Garcia, Mayte Weitzman, and Lizette Trujillo of AeroMexico.

A special thanks to friends and associates who gave insightful advice and help. Among them are Rene Bustamente, Pierre and Marieke Baumgartner, Ricky Wilson, G. P. Shryer, Cathleen Tilley, Ellen Zimmerli, Jim and Kelly Luedeke, Ron Slaughter, Rocky Behr, José Rodriguez, Dr. and Mrs. Karl Butzer, Rhonda Gainer, Jonny Boyd, George W. Romer, Howard and Beverly Karno, Rosie Garcia, Chuck and Dev Stern, Chris Carson, Mike Roberts, Janine Manjaris, Mike Titsworth, Gary and Carol Flake, Carmen Haddon, Bertha Cardenas, Doug Burdge, Merrick Bonewitz, Luther Wilson, Ralph Hurd, Virginia de Barrios, Tom Wuelpern, and Elaine Paul. Our deep appreciation to Fonda San Miguel owner Tom Gilliland, Chef Roberto Santibañez, and Diana Kennedy.

Finally, we extend our sincere gratitude to our families for their constant support—my mother, Judith M. Simpson, and sisters, Amy Witynski Holmes, Mara Witynski, and Jenny Witynski. And a heartfelt thank you to Joe P. Carr Sr. and Joe P. Carr III for their special support.

To AeroMexico
for their continued support
and for providing us with air transportation
during our research trips to Mexico.

CONTENTS

FOREWORD

Growing up in Mexico as a child, I was repeatedly told that Mexico was a cornucopia of abundance with all sorts of fruits, vegetables, and grains spilling out of the mythical horn. Teachers would even point out how the shape of the Mexico map resembled the fabled horn of abundance. One of the untapped riches of Mexico that surely needs to be included as part of the country's abundance is its legacy of architecture. From the pre-Hispanic monuments through colonial magnificence to today's vibrant modern Mexican movement, the architecture of Mexico is truly one of its unique riches.

A main component of Mexico's rich architectural heritage is, of course, what Karen and Joe are so beautifully presenting in the theme of this book—the hacienda and its rich design style.

With advancement through the ages and changes in the economy, land tenure, and the onslaught of the modern industrial age, the hacienda system of production became obsolete and most of these sprawling architectural complexes were abandoned. Except for a few outstanding examples whose owners have heroically maintained their ancestral inheritance into modern times, hacienda complexes had fallen into dismal abandonment and disrepair.

Luckily for Mexico and the rest of the world, there is a strong movement afoot, mostly by private individuals and institutions, to salvage these architectural wonders that hark to a bygone era.

With a strong vision, hefty investment of funds and time, and, above all, the creative juices that fuel these endeavors, the haciendas that dot the varied Mexican landscape are being rescued from the jaws of destruction and neglect and lovingly brought back to their former glory. This labor of love is happening not a moment too soon.

Haciendas can be found throughout Mexico and vary according to their purpose. From the cattle and mining operations in arid desert regions to the north, to the coffee plantations of the Chiapas lowlands; from the mining enterprises found in the mountains of Guanajuato, to the *henequén* plantations in Yucatán; from the *pulque* palaces of the highland plains, to flamboyant sugar *ingenios* of Morelos with imposing *chacuaco* smokestacks piercing the skies and visible for many a league in the distant landscape, Mexican haciendas are many and varied.

Haciendas in Mexico were built through a span of four centuries. Their architectural styles reflect the style in vogue at the time they were built, along with the technology and building materials available in the region. The baroque exuberance of La Casa de los Perros in Apaseo del Alto in Guanajuato or the serene splendor of San Gabriel de las Palmas, the eclecticism expressed by the fantasies of the owners of the late-nineteenth-century pulque haciendas of Hidalgo and the henequén haciendas of Yucatán, where seemingly landed estates of neo-

Gothic castles are just a few pastures apart from a French rococo—these examples give us a glimpse of the range of architectural styles one can encounter when trying to classify haciendas according to style.

The abundance of historic architecture in Mexico has spawned a new style, a new movement—one that rescues old buildings and makes them useful again, one that delights us with time-proven beauty and allows us to touch the past. By rebuilding this wonderful architectural heritage, age-old furnishings and crafts are continued or revived and integrated into modern times. The eloquence and virtuosity are here to embrace the human spirit.

In order to find new uses for these splendid sprawling spectacles, the new owners of haciendas have to energize their imaginations and temper their desires. Introducing bamboo crops is Yucatán's Hacienda Xixim; some are exclusive resorts like Hacienda San Gabriel de las Palmas or private villas like Hacienda Cuatitla. Others are orphanages or corporate retreats, schools or museums. Youth training camps like Hacienda Tabi are evidence that imagination has no limits on how to adapt and reuse this vast architectural legacy.

In some cases it is the surrounding community of humble means that has undertaken the responsibility of rescuing a hacienda and making it work for the community as a source of employment. Hacienda Xaaga in Oaxaca, for example, is being turned into a museum of architectural history. It boasts of buildings ranging from a pre-Hispanic Zapotec elite tomb to an early-twentieth-century grain silo. At Hacienda Cetelac in Yaxuna, Yucatán, the community will restore the building to form a multilingual school and community center, benefiting locals and foreigners alike.

Showing the way and leaders of this movement are people and institutions that include Roberto Hernández, the Rodolfo Morales Foundation, and Manuel Serrano, whose skill and dedication to the rescue of historic haciendas has spurned the imagination of nationals and foreigners to discover, rescue, and enjoy these wonderful architectural treasures.

—Eugen Logan Wagner, Ph.D., AIA.

INTRODUCTION

HIDDEN IN IDYLLIC ISOLATION, THE HACIENDAS OF OLD MEXICO HAVE DETERIORATED IN A PHOTOGENIC WAY. WALLS EXPOSED TO CENTURIES OF WEATHER AND WEAR HAVE FADED FROM CRIMSON TO PINK, REVEALING AS MANY TEXTURES AS A JULIAN SCHNABEL PAINTING. Grand-scale interiors—once overgrown with towering trees and crumbling floral frescoes—now invite contemporary furniture to contrast with their original stone walls; a maze of ancient aqueducts are newly configured to become garden waterfalls; and *casa de máquinas*, or machine houses, have been restored as artists' homes and sculptural backdrops to sparkling new pools.

The rich imagery of the hacienda and its newly restored forms were the inspiration for this volume. Our first book, *Mexican Country Style*, unveiled country antiques and architectural elements in their original contexts, as well as their newfound roles in contemporary interiors. Our continued fascination with Mexico's artful traditions has led us on a twenty-year journey throughout Mexico's rural landscape.

Over the last five years, we have witnessed a widespread preservation movement that has gained great momentum in Mexico, stimulating a revival of traditional construction techniques—from carved stone, adobe, and *bóvedas* (vaulted ceilings), to *tapial* (rammed earth) and stucco textures enhanced by the use of cactus juice. Accompanying this revival is a heightened interest in colonial antiques, artifacts, and accents attractive in their embodiment of an era of craftsmanship that contrasts sharply with our own. A fascinating hybrid of Spanish and Mexican traditions, the Mexican hacienda has been a captivating source of design inspiration for over three centuries. Following the Mexican Revolution

One of Yucatán's largest henequén estates, Hacienda Yaxcopoil originally occupied 22,000 acres and is presently a museum.

Opposite: A tribute to minimal Mexican design, an antique balance hangs as a sculptural counterpoint to an old colonial trunk.

Above: Stacked ceramic roof tiles fill a deserted hacienda doorway awaiting restoration.

of 1910, many haciendas were abandoned or left to decay, suspended between a past memory and an unknown future. Today, these architectural treasures have been rediscovered by a new generation of international designers, architects, and preservationists. Thanks to innovative restoration efforts, the hacienda has been adapted to myriad new uses, and its visual culture has sparked design inspiration on both sides of the border.

Heralding a new era in Mexican design, the "new hacienda" brings together an intriguing mix of centuries-old traditions with contemporary design in its modern adaptations. From country homes for artists and filmmakers to eco-conscious resorts, restaurants, art centers, and riding schools, the hacienda has transformed tradition to become a part of modern-day life.

Designed for self-sufficiency, haciendas were the economic backbone of rural Mexico from Conquest to Revolution. According to their moment in time, they encompassed a variety of architectural and interior styles. In the early sixteenth and seventeenth centuries, the majority of haciendas were modest in dimension and interiors were austere, with Spanish-influenced, locally crafted furniture. In the prosperous sugar and mining regions, however, hacienda interiors began to reflect luxurious European influences earlier than the more isolated estates.

As the hacienda system began to grow and prosper in the eighteenth century, hacienda owners were influenced by European furniture styles and self-indulgent foreign travels. As a result, Spanish, Italian, and French furnishings soon resided with Mexican-country pieces and generations of family heirlooms. This mix of rural and sophisticated elements became a common sight throughout the countryside. In the late nineteenth century, the haciendas reached the height of their splendor during the *Porfiriato*, the period from 1876 to 1911, which marked the successive terms of President Porfirio Díaz.

During his reign, Díaz restored economic strength to the country and fostered the rise of foreign investment and large-scale landholding. Thus, an emphasis on decoration became popular. Not surprisingly, many haciendas from this period drew inspiration from other lands and other ages. Many *hacendados* (hacienda owners) opted to incorporate Moorish elements into traditional Spanish styles. Others chose French-style châteaux, Italian palazzos, Renaissance villas, or Victorian Gothic mansions. Dotting the Mexican landscape with their minarets and pointed arches, these later haciendas resembled medieval European castles.

Above and beyond the normal trappings of earlier hacienda periods, the Porfiriato ushered in extensive face-lifts and expansions for leisure activities: ballrooms, bullrings, bowling alleys, sewing rooms, libraries, small theaters, swimming pools, observatories, and sometimes even a family museum.

Hacienda Lencero, nestled in the town of Jalapa in Veracruz, was the former home of Antonio Lopez Santa Anna, the eleven-time president of Mexico. In 1981, the state of Veracruz purchased the sprawling property and converted it to the Museo de Muebles, or Furniture Museum. Rooms are filled with furnishings from Mexico, Europe, and Asia, showcasing the elegant style found in Mexico during the nineteenth century. One of the more fascinating pieces of furniture is the leader's original bed, embellished with the national emblem of an eagle holding a snake in its beak. The country estate is also noted for its two-storied

An old jail door contrasts sharply with the ornately stenciled wall decorating this recently restored space in Ocotlán.

arched veranda, neoclassical-style chapel, and rectangular lake, complete with black and white swans.

Over the years, our decades of furniture research provided us with serendipitous hacienda visits and the opportunity to study the diversity of their design styles. From the tropical coffee-growing mountains in Oaxaca to vast cattle-grazing lands in Durango, our travels led us to wildly remote regions and ultimately to hidden storage buildings and barns still in use on deserted haciendas.

Intrigued by the gracefully told stories of witty farmers and local historians, we were propelled forward on our quest for more hacienda lore. We discovered it was not unusual for many haciendas to have had former lives as barracks, hospitals, schools, storage areas, or even orphanages.

LORE

In the early nineties, our first hacienda visit captured our attention. It was a late summer afternoon in a small village outside of Tlaxcala. Our trek that day was originally intended to view an old *dispensario*, or grain storage trunk, supposedly stored in a nearby stable. The trunk surfaced and—thanks to its location—so did our passion for the monuments of Mexico's past.

We were transported to another time and place as we approached the remains of a seventeenth-century *pulque* hacienda. From a distance, endless rows of agaves surrounded the austere, fortress-like compound. The agaves' pointy crowns spread dramatic shadows across the towering white facade, reminding us of the hacienda's once-important production of pulque, the fermented juice of the maguey, which includes several varieties of the agave.

Once inside, we were greeted by browsing goats and a strong silence that invited contemplation. The entire *casco*, or hacienda complex, had a sense of austerity that was monastic yet modern. From the center of the courtyard we faced the *casa grande*, or main house, and its attached chapel with arched bell screen. Nearby were stables, corrals, buildings for administration and storage, the *tinacal*, or pulque-making hall, and housing for permanent workers.

Our curiosity ushered us down the arcaded portals and into grand salons and drawing rooms. To our surprise, they had become storerooms for livestock supplies. Inside, long shadows followed as we entered doorless doorways. Remnants of rustic furniture were scattered about: wooden ranch chairs sat beneath a suit of Spanish armor, topped with an

Right: The subtle textures of stone, carved wood and adobe are ever-present in many forms.

old Revolutionary sombrero; an old stone water filter was half hidden by stacks of hay; and a crumbling stuccoed wall displayed an empty antique picture frame filled with lace-like cobwebs. Whose portrait was missing?

Our wandering continued and led us to the tinacal, where huge fermentation vats sat empty on large wooden supports and a painted mural dressed the barren wall. The mural depicted the ever-present maguey plant, dotting the landscape in once-vivid colors. It was barren and beautiful.

Over the next few years, our hacienda visits increased as we sought to learn more about regional design differences. Eerily deserted but alive with incredible craftsmanship were the spaces used for family gathering and resting, along with the chapel, the jail, and the gardens. These features had an astounding diversity and vitality of architectural ornament: stone-chinked walls, bóvedas, stone moldings, finials, and iron window grilles. The richness in craftsmanship conjured images of their original environments.

For us, the hacienda became a lens through which to view Mexico's past. Avid readers of Mexican history, we also added film research to our study. In the 1949 film *Veracruz*, Gary Cooper and Burt Lancaster led us behind the fortress-like walls of Veracruz haciendas for a close-up look at grand-scale architecture. Sergei Eisenstein's *¡Qué Viva México!* brought Hidalgo's Hacienda Tetlapayac to life through its vivid images of a working hacienda in the 1930s. Paradoxically, Tetlapayac's workers were used as extras and the hacendado made a cameo appearance, although the film harshly criticized the hacienda system's treatment of peóns. Harrison Ford even helped us get an intimate look at the magnificent sugar hacienda San Gabriel de las Palmas in the state of Morelos through his adventures in the film *Clear and Present Danger*.

We were further inspired by two impressive volumes produced by Fomento Cultural Banamex, A.C., published in Mexico in the nineties. *Haciendas of Mexico* and *Daily Life on the Haciendas of Mexico* provided us with a comprehensive look at hacienda architectural styles and vivid historical accounts of hacienda daily life, including celebrations, religious practices, and amusements.

By the mid-nineties our travels revealed more and more country estates undergoing restoration, being readied for extended lives as country homes, art studios, exotic plant nurseries, health spas, educational retreats, and hotels/restaurants.

Left: Beautiful murals surround the pulque fermentation vats at Hacienda Tetlapayac. Courtesy Las Haciendas de Hidalgo.

One of the more historically fascinating properties to make the transition to hacienda/hotel is the Hacienda Cortés in Cuernavaca. Built in the sixteenth century to house Mexico's conqueror, the luxury estate was renovated and opened in 1981. Its outdoor areas are simple and magical. The open-air restaurant is surrounded by ancient stone walls crawling with massive tree roots, and its swimming pool sits in the center of tall stone columns of the former structure. Another estate that has made a beautiful transition to resort is Hacienda San Miguel Regla, a once-prosperous silver mining hacienda in Hidalgo with an impressive stone aqueduct and seventeenth-century chapel. Additionally, Plan Group Hotels completed luxurious renovations of three key haciendas in the Yucatán— Temozón, Santa Rosa, and San José. Visionaries in hacienda design and adaptive reuse, their work expresses a unique design sense, combining vivid color, a mix of antique and modern furnishings, and an air of noble simplicity.

On the artistic front, a former silver-ore-processing hacienda has been restored as the Silver Center of Zacatecas. There, the region's centuries-old traditions are kept alive as the center trains first-class craftsmen in jewelry making and silversmithing. In the Yucatán, two artists have created a dramatic home and art studio in an old casa de máquinas of the former henequén hacienda Sacchich. Another old henequén estate has been revived to house a certified coconut-palm plantation, where special hybrids are raised. Hacienda San Antonio Chalanté in Izamal has added artful equestrian traditions to the hotel property with its extensive riding trails and instruction, and in Colima, a private hacienda is home to an impressive antique-car collection, featuring over a hundred American cars from the 1920s and 1930s.

In Oaxaca, our travels uncovered the great richness of the region's old agricultural haciendas. Nestled among the hills surrounding the city of Oaxaca, many of the estate's old *molinos*, or mills that once ground wheat, have been innovatively restored. One in particular, best known in the Etla Valley for its former production of *pan armarillo*, or yellow bread, heralds its past in an artistic new way. Two massive millstones are now inset into the adobe entrance wall. Oaxaca, we discovered, had also become a leader of the architectural-preservation movement, thanks to the efforts of two prominent artists: Francisco Toledo and Rodolfo Morales. Their efforts included the rescue and restoration of numerous colonial buildings and haciendas for future generations to enjoy.

Nestled in the shadow of two volcanoes is the Hacienda de San Antonio, a former coffee hacienda that has survived both a revolution and volcanic eruption. Something of a

miracle, the nineteenth-century hacienda has persevered to become a newly restored executive retreat in Colima. Surrounded by a dramatic volcanic rock aqueduct—built to water the estate's coffee and sugarcane fields—the property's newest additions include a fifty-foot swimming pool, outdoor dining area, and private amphitheater.

In the heart of the Coahuila desert, the 400-year-old Hacienda San Lorenzo has evolved gracefully over time and is home to the oldest winery in Mexico. Originating with a land grant from King Philip in 1597, San Lorenzo continues to produce wine in its Madero winery. The owners, who are descendants of revolutionary hero Francisco Madero, have recently updated the hacienda to add hotel/restaurant facilities for visitors to this historical town, Parras de la Fuentes.

A trip to the Yucatán also continued to enrich our hacienda experience. The mysterious Mayan region abounds not only with dozens of ancient cities, but a magnificent concentration of haciendas. They combine in their history the three great periods of ancient Yucatán: the pre-Columbian period, the time of the Spanish colony, and the henequén boom years of the late-nineteenth and early-twentieth century. Cultivated and exported for rope and twine, the henequén crop produced great wealth for the region's hacienda owners, who nicknamed their crop "green gold."

With an extension of 22,000 acres in its time of greatest splendor, Hacienda Yaxcopoil is considered one of Yucatán's most important rural estates because of its size and historic importance in both the cattle and sisal industries. Now a museum, the *casa principal*, or main house, features spacious corridors, and high-ceilinged drawing rooms display the estate's impressive collection of original furniture, oil paintings, and everyday objects, including books, maps, and ancient pottery found among Mayan ruins on the property. Needless to say, the mix of European furniture and Mayan artifacts successfully creates a vivid atmosphere of the period.

By contrast, our first new hacienda visit was alive with the comforts and conveniences of modern-day life, yet its soulful past was ever present. Owned by Robert Gow, an American businessman, Hacienda Xixim, also located on the Yucatán peninsula, was recently transformed from an abandoned sixteenth-century cattle hacienda into a thriving bamboo plantation and restful home retreat. The property was beautifully adapted to its current business/home use and displays artful bamboo furnishings as reminders of its current livelihood. The hacienda's original *norias*, or wells, are utilized to water the fields, and local Mayan Indians—preferring to

Opposite: An intricately carved comoda is brightened by Alberto Monta's painting. The lamps, newly converted from molasses storage jars, are topped with sterling silver shades. Collection of Ed Holler and Sam Saunders.

Below: This rinconera, or corner table, reflects the French influence in Mexican design during the reign of Emperor Maximilian. Collection of Jack Dulaney.

live and work near their ancestral homes—are employed to harvest and craft the mature bamboo into decorative gates and furnishings.

As we enter the new millennium, the hacienda lives on in its newly adapted forms as well as in new interpretations outside its country of origin. Integrating easily into California and the American Southwest, the hacienda's familiar silhouette—arcaded portals and interior courtyards—are ideally suited to warm-weather climates.

On both sides of the border, a new generation of designers and architects have found inspiration in the hacienda's visual culture and have integrated its signature use of natural materials and Mexican furnishings into new homes.

Overlooking the Pacific Ocean, a hacienda-style home in Pacific Palisades, California, has integrated Mexican stone, furniture, tile, and hand-hewn wood beams into its design. Hidden in the Tucson desert, a new hacienda features massive mesquite *portones*, or entrance doors, stone surrounds for windows and doorways, and an awe-inspiring 60' x 60' courtyard. On the West Coast, architect Douglas W. Burdge and designer Sarah Bartlett have incorporated Mexican design elements into hacienda-style homes throughout Cabo San Lucas, Baja California, and southern California. In West Texas, an intriguing adaptation to a historic fortress was completed by architect Chris Carson of Ford, Powell, and Carson, who created a contemporary mix between hacienda architectural details and Mexican furnishings within an austere rustic landscape.

As Mexico's restoration movement continues, the new millennium will see many more haciendas rediscovered and rescued. At present, there are countless haciendas and colonial homes in the planning stages of restoration, many of which we have viewed in their gracefully decaying state. In a few short years, their renovations will be complete and their histories preserved. Importantly, efforts are being made to integrate the villages and communities into the restoration of their historical structures. By teaching local youths preservation techniques in stone, adobe, plaster, wood-carving, and iron, traditions are being kept alive so that future generations may be involved in the preservation and maintenance of their architectural and artistic patrimony.

We look forward with great anticipation to the emerging presence of Mexico's new haciendas and the continued spark of inspiration they provide worldwide.

HACIENDA ORIGINS

"FROM A DISTANCE THE EXTENSIVE HABITATION HAS A STATELY AIR, LIKE SOME DUCAL RESIDENCE. IN APPROACHING IT YOU PASS FIRST THROUGH FIELDS OF MAGUEY AND BLOSSOMING ALFALFA, THEN BY A LONG STONE CORRAL FOR CATTLE, EXTENSIVE BARRACKS and huts of laborers, and a pond bordered with weeping willows. It is built of rubble-masonry and plaster, whitewashed, and consists of a single liberal story. The dwelling, with numerous connected buildings, makes in all a facade of about six hundred feet. A belfry, with two tiers of bronze bells hung in arches, sets off the center. The large windows are defended by cage-like iron gratings. A door, flanked by holy-water fonts, at the left of that forming the main entrance, opens into a family chapel. In a gable above the main entrance is inscribed this motto — which has not, however, prevented the hacienda from being the scene of more than one sack by revolutionary forces: 'En aqueste destierro y soledad disfruto del tesoro de la paz,' or 'In this retirement and solitude I enjoy the treasure of peace.'"

— William Henry Bishop, 1890s

Layer upon layer, century by century, the hacienda has continuously evolved through the ups and downs of Mexico's rich history. First appearing in New Spain shortly after the Conquest (1521), the haciendas began as land grants awarded by the king of Spain to local conquistadors and Spanish notables in exchange for military and social services to the crown. For over three hundred years the haciendas were the economic backbone of rural Mexico from Conquest to Revolution. The term *hacienda* is derived from the Spanish verb *hacer*, to do, with a primary meaning of "a profit-making or income-

Hacienda San Ysidro rises like a medieval European castle amid a mass of nopales. Courtesy Mariana Yampolsky.

producing enterprise." The traditional hacienda was an estate that belonged to a recognized member of a privileged elite and whose economic activity took place in the agricultural sector from agriculture, livestock, mining, or manufacture. It revolved around natural resources, an organized labor force, and commercial systems.

Although some estates operated with modest acreage, over time many *hacendados*, or hacienda owners, acquired multiple properties, either through direct purchase or by appropriating Indian land.

REGIONAL DIVERSITY

According to their moment in time, climate, and terrain, Mexico's haciendas were quite diverse in architectural design and kind of production. Although some estates encompassed several operations, most derived their earnings from a single source. As

Right: An early engraving of Hacienda Tepenacasco in Hidalgo features an imposing espadana, or arch-pierced bell screen. The inscription over the entrance reads, "In this refinement and solitude I enjoy the treasure of peace."

noted by Mexico's historian of the haciendas, Gisela von Wobeser, in Paul Alexander Bartlett's *The Haciendas of Mexico*, there were three principal types of haciendas. "The grain haciendas were the most important as they cultivated the basic crops (corn, wheat, beans, and chiles). These estates were located near urban centers, including Puebla, Toluca, Oaxaca, Guadalajara, and Michoacán. Livestock haciendas were second in importance and raised cattle, goats, and sheep on the vast lands in northern Mexico. Farther south, the tropical regions of Veracruz, Morelos, and Cuernavaca were host to the grand-scale sugar haciendas where water was plentiful for sugarcane cultivation."

28

Also of note, the mountainous areas of Zacatecas, Guanajuato, and San Luis Potosí gave birth to prosperous silver-mining haciendas where ore was extracted and refined. Coffee, vanilla, cacao, rubber, and exotic hardwoods were also harvested in a variety of tropical regions. The states of Mexico, Hidalgo, and Tlaxcala favored the production of *pulque*, the intoxicating drink made since pre-Hispanic times by fermenting the sweet sap of the maguey plant. In the Yucatán, the hacendados acquired great wealth and recognition from the cultivation and export of *henequén*, or sisal, during the green gold boom of the late-nineteenth and early-twentieth centuries. A bluish green, fibrous member of the agave family, henequén is native to the Yucatán peninsula and was harvested before the Conquest by the Maya for use as rope, hammocks, textiles, and mats.

THE CASCO

Isolated by their own magnitude, haciendas became self-sufficient communities unto themselves. Protected by extensive walls, the *casco* was the heart of the hacienda. It consisted of the *casa grande*, or main house, and a complex arrangement of buildings and open spaces that included the hacienda's chapel, barns, corrals, stables, granaries, silos, workshops, workers' quarters, and *tienda de raya*, or general store, where merchandise was

Opposite: The bedroom at Hacienda Chimalpa in Hidalgo gives new meaning to grand scale with its ornately gilted mirror. Courtesy Las Haciendas de Hidalgo.

Above: In a bedroom at Hacienda Ocotepec, Hidalgo, walls feature imported floral wallpaper, and a water jug made of fine china. Courtesy Mariana Yampolsky.

sold. The importance of the productive aspect of the hacienda was evident in the closeness between the main house and the outbuildings. Many included their own stone quarries, brick kilns, iron forges, and tanneries. A complex system of aqueducts, dams, and reservoirs kept the estate supplied with water.

Not only was the casco the productive and architectural center, it was also the heart of the hacienda's day-to-day life. In feudal style, workers, or *peóns*, were forced by low wages to contract debts, which bound them to the hacienda for the rest of their lives.

THE EARLY PERIOD

In the early colonial period, most haciendas were constructed in modest dimensions appropriate to the needs for living and working. Most often, the casa grande was built as a single story, featuring *bóvedas*, or high vaulted ceilings, and quality materials but with little ornamentation. The hacienda continued to grow in size as uncultivated land was transformed into farmland and water distribution systems opened up new areas to irrigation. Because of increases in production and population, the early-sixteenth-century facilities began to grow and were expanded in later decades, eventually becoming extensive estates that revealed influences from a number of periods. Over the years, hacienda buildings were modified and boundaries redrawn as family fortunes waxed and waned.

THE PORFIRIATO PERIOD

During the second half of the nineteenth century, many haciendas were modernized or totally rebuilt, reflecting the technological advances and increases in hacienda production and population of workers.

The haciendas achieved their maximum splendor during the Porfiriato, the period from 1876 to 1911, which marked the successive terms of President Porfirio Díaz. Through the use of capitalistic measures, Díaz restored economic strength to the country by encouraging European and American investment and developing industry and transportation, thus steering Mexico into the twentieth century. Earlier in the nineteenth century, there had been failed attempts by liberals to dissolve the hacienda and restore the land to the Indians. Díaz did the opposite; he encouraged large-scale landholdings and provided extra land to establish new haciendas. As many haciendas underwent extensive face-lifts to reflect the new national confidence, an emphasis on elaborate decoration became popular.

Despite their isolated locations, hacienda interiors boasted a surprising degree of influence from European and Asian cultures.

Toward the end of the Porfiriato, the architecture became proportionately immense and ostentatious. Many newly constructed haciendas drew inspiration from other lands and other ages. Rising amidst the Mexican countryside of magueys and *nopal* cactus were French-style châteaux, Italian palazzos, and Victorian Gothic mansions. As this period brought lavish entertaining and regular visits from dignitaries and foreigners, the addition of private amphitheaters, bullrings, ballrooms, recital halls, and even observatories was common. The casco was also the site of the hacienda's many fiestas. Here the hacendado openly displayed his wealth and hosted gallant displays of the arts of the Mexican horseman, or *charro*, bullfights, and festive dances.

MEXICAN REVOLUTION AND AGRARIAN REFORM

In 1821, Mexico gained independence from Spain; however, it did not bring tranquillity. A long period of turbulence and political instability followed as the presidency changed

hands thirty-six times between 1833 and 1855. Soon after, the French occupied Mexico from 1864 to 1867, with Maximilian and his wife, Carlotta, installed as emperor and empress. Although this intervention was brief, it began a period of French influence in architecture and culture that lasted well into the twentieth century.

By 1876, the Mexicans again took control of their own country with General Porfirio Díaz serving thirty years as president. His reign gave rise to a new aristocracy characterized by tremendous landholdings and opulent influences. The excesses of this period and the resulting inequality between the classes triggered the 1910 Mexican Revolution. Under the leadership of such legendary figures as Emiliano Zapata and Pancho Villa, the struggle continued until 1920, with bands of rebels looting and burning haciendas across the country. By 1934, a new political party ushered in a period of political stability with the election of President Lázaro Cárdenas.

The hacienda began its passage into history as the Agrarian Land Reform Act abolished the feudal hacienda system. Estates were reduced to a collection of structures amidst a multitude of land parcels. The servile bonds that had tied peóns to the hacienda were finally broken.

In the summer of 1938, President Cárdenas wrote to his American friend William C. Townsend: "We are confident that the people and the government of the United States will be able to grasp the fact that the breaking up of the large estates is the main point in our national program for improving the living conditions of the peasants of Mexico. The idea of

giving land to the masses was written into the Constitution at the cost of much bloodshed and my government is duty-bound to comply with that mandate. All the holdings that are larger than what the Agrarian Code permits are subject to distribution if there are peasants nearby who do not have land to till. Each landowner, however, is permitted to retain 370 acres, whether he is a foreigner or a Mexican."

By 1945, approximately forty-five million acres of hacienda land had been turned over to the homeless and the landless by President Cárdenas. Three hundred haciendas in the country could claim more than one million acres apiece and then only for a brief period.

Major monuments to a fascinating era, Mexico's haciendas are proving indestructible. Although not all have survived intact, a vast number are being rescued and revived for new lives in a new millennium. Thanks to the recent Mexican preservation movement that has focused attention on colonial buildings and haciendas, a new generation of architects, designers, and preservationists are protecting Mexico's rich design history for future generations to enjoy.

FURNISHINGS AND ACCENTS

THE NEW HACIENDA DESIGN STYLE OFFERS A TANGIBLE LINK TO MEXICO'S PAST WITH A FOCUS ON THE USE OF NATURAL MATERIALS, RICH ARCHITECTURAL ELEMENTS, TEXTURES, AND ARTIFACTS. AS THE HACIENDA ENTERS YET ANOTHER CENTURY, ITS TRADITIONAL silhouette continues to capture our attention, evolving and absorbing new influences. Colonial antiques and country objects are intermingled with contemporary notions of art and comfort, maintaining a balance between looking back and forging ahead.

Rooms are a study in travel and time. From Spain, France, Asia — and back home to Mexico — the juxtapositions are elegantly simple and often full of surprise. Unexpected elements spiral out of the commonplace to ornament interiors with wit and charm. Old trunk *chapas*, or lock plates, displayed in multiples become a new art form against an exposed adobe wall. Inset in garden walls, heavy millstones once used to crush wheat now announce their past; an ancient iron balance evolves as sculpture when hung over a colonial trunk.

Behind massive stone walls and observation towers, hacienda interiors have had an elusive image over the last three centuries. It's no wonder. Their passage through history has traced striking contradictions in design style, resulting in interior atmospheres of rustic austerity to more formal European extravagances. Many haciendas were burned or looted of their furnishings during the revolutionary years. Some, however, survived intact either by luck or by virtue of their remote location. In spite of their individual ups and downs, all haciendas experienced periodic changes as time and

A colonial bench resides with a modern blue sphere and wooden candlesticks. Collection of Holler and Saunders.

modern advances brought new preferences. A blend of old and new, rustic and formal have established quarters under the same roof.

The media of history and cinema have transmitted images that generally portray Mexico's noble country estates as grand-scale salons filled with colonial art, antiques, pianos, and billiard tables—definitive trappings of a privileged elite. Certainly this is reflective of the Porfiriato period, 1876 to 1911, when the haciendas had reached the height of their splendor. Interestingly, this is not the state in which they were always found.

Depending on the moment in time and the owner's taste, hacienda interiors encompassed a variety of design themes. In the early sixteenth and seventeenth centuries, with the exception of the grand sugar and mining estates, hacienda interiors were typically austere, as the *casa grande* was built in modest dimensions and geared towards the working life. During this period, many wealthy landowners preferred life in the cities and rarely lived full time on their estates. During the reign of Porfirio Díaz, Mexico became more politically stable and the countryside was free of raiding banditos. Now able to freely traverse the countryside in their caravans of carriages, *hacendados*, or hacienda owners, spent more time on their haciendas, consequently furnishing their homes with comforts and luxuries to enable extended stays and regular entertaining.

Because of their isolation, haciendas were almost totally self-sufficient, incorporating carpentry workshops for making furniture, doors, shutters, corral gates, carts, wheels, farm implements, and even religious *santos*, or saints—basically whatever daily life required. Carpenters crafted functional and rustic-style furniture from locally available woods, using Spanish-style furnishings as their inspiration.

Hacienda owners often commissioned Spanish-style armoires, benches, chairs, and tables from the carpentry workshops in Mexico City. These pieces eventually made their way from town homes and mansions to the country estates. From these examples, hacienda carpenters adapted specific details—raised panels on armoires, scalloped rails or spindles on benches, and turned table legs—but often in a more simplified form.

A number of accounts exist that speak of the sobriety characterizing the haciendas during their early period. Madame Calderón de la Barca, wife of Spain's first ambassador to Mexico, left this account of a hacienda in Tacubaya during her travels in 1840.

The house . . . is generally a large empty building, with innumerable lofty

rooms, communicating with each other, and containing the scantiest possible supply

Opposite: Argentine maté cups decorate an early Spanish table, beside it a classic hip-joint chair. Collection of Fred Pottinger.

Above: A colonial armario, or armoire, features raised panels in a diamond design.

38

of furniture. One room will have in it a deal table and a few chairs; you will then pass through five or six quite empty; then you will arrive at two or three, with green painted bedsteads and a bench; the walls bare or ornamented with a few old pictures of Saints and Virgins, and bare floors ornamented with nothing. . . . Such are most of the haciendas that I have yet seen.

By contrast, the Hernán Cortés hacienda, former home to the famed conqueror, is described by Mrs. Alec-Tweedie during her Cuernavaca visit to the noble estate in 1901.

It is the dearest old place; so strong and massive, so imposing in its solid strength. . . . The buildings run all round four sides of an enormous courtyard. In the rooms are some of Cortés's massive wooden chests, one of which is big enough to have comfortably held the lady of whom we read in the "Mistletoe Bough." Below the apartments are great dark cellars, which form a sort of cloister, where the sugar is extracted from the molasses. . . . The whole place was teeming with poetry and romance; every corner was a picture, every room contained enough subject matter to fill a volume. Intrigue, conspiracy, murder, all lay hidden in the silent stones of those great walls and arched domes.

Inventories compiled in 1549 from the Cortés home enumerate the items found in luxury dwellings of that era. As reported by Francisco Garabana: "Gold tableware, Flemish tapestries, oriental rugs, and embossed leathers were of primary importance after which came a few general types of furniture. Chairs and benches, tables and beds; bureaus, chests, armoires, and strong boxes were among those pieces mentioned, with a variety of style and workmanship depicted in each category."

The Spanish period continued to see a hybrid style evolve as native designs were incorporated into imported colonial patterns. Carved, decorative ornaments such as birds and grapevines were used, mingled with the foliated cross, the monogram of Christ, and the leaf-shaped heart. Motifs of Aztec or Inca origin crept into the work of indigenous craftsmen. Favorites included the Inca sun and snake. Christian saints were depicted with Indian faces, and symbols of the Passion often echoed pre-Conquest designs.

Oriental styles began to affect colonial furniture after 1565, when a trade route was initiated between the Philippines and Acapulco. In the early 1600s, luxury furniture imported for privileged officials began to reflect the baroque, and, soon after, the movement gradually appeared in the domestic furnishings of the town homes and haciendas.

Hacienda San José Huejotzingo, in Puebla, was visited by artist Paul Alexander Bartlett in the 1940s and he describes its post-Revolutionary condition. "Destroyed by revolutionaries, its chapel and storage areas are roofless, but the residential rooms have been reconditioned. They are filled with *recuerdos* [mementos]: Incunabula, antique firearms, a suit of Italian armor, oil paintings, Aztec figures, charro spurs, leather chests,

An eighteenth-century Mexican Chippendale armario topped with American Indian baskets anchors one corner of the Pottinger living room. A European carved-wood archbishop stands close by.

40

colonial tables and chairs. In the dining room are tall ecclesiastical wooden candelabra, carved cedar chairs, monogrammed chests, pre-Columbian objects, colonial pottery and old dishes. Modern Tónala pottery ornaments a nineteenth-century buffet."

The chest was one of the most indispensable early pieces of furniture, and it took many forms. Strongboxes were made with thick wood slabs and lined with iron bars. Large trunks for storing valuables, especially those belonging to institutions, had three *chapas*, or locks, so three separate keys could be distributed to different individuals to assure honesty and security. Most lock plates were decorated with scrolled outlines and engraved with motifs such as exotic birds or rosettes.

Later examples of nineteenth-century Mexican chests featured impressive marquetry and inlay work in a variety of woods—mahogany, lemonwood, walnut, cypress—over a pine base. Motifs included floral scrolls, tendrils, ribbons, and birds. The *concha*, or shell design, was a favorite motif used abundantly in Mexican design.

Vargueños, or traveling desks, were highly prized possessions for storing valuables and important papers. Easily transportable, these small storage cabinets were designed with highly decorated drawers and a locking fall front, which also served as a writing surface. When open, vargueño covers were supported by sliding brackets that pulled out of a stand, usually a *pie de puente*, or trestle table. Although its origins lie in Spain and Italy, the vargueño was also made in Mexico and other Latin American countries. Today they remain one of the most highly cherished family pieces and are noted for their extensive ivory inlay work and gold-leaf moldings.

Throughout the colonial period, the bench was a familiar sight in the portals and long corridors of convents, municipal buildings, and haciendas. From the early hearty styles with single slab planks and large *clavos*, to the more ornately carved and spindled examples, benches reflected the influences of the period and available natural resources.

Many estates featured built-in masonry benches in front or inside the main hacienda entrance since they were often used by riders dismounting. Other built-in benches were plastered and decoratively painted or intricately tiled.

Early chair styles included the sixteenth-century *sillón de cadera* (X-chair), or hip-joint chair, which has its origins in the Italian Renaissance. It was favored for its ease in folding and transport. Another classic chair that had a Mexican presence is the sixteenth-century Spanish *sillón de frailero*, or friar's chair. Featuring straight lines, the stretched leather seat and back were held together with brass nails. Its standard shape was square,

Opposite: A carved Chinese falcon watches over the entrance to the grand salon of the Sibley home.

Above: An elaborately decorated vargueño, or traveling desk, from Spain decorates the Sibley home.

although more sophisticated turnings and carving were seen later in the seventeenth century. The traditional sillón also was common, featuring scrolled and curved arms and fluted legs. On the simpler end of the spectrum, other favored chairs included the *butaca*, or leather sling chair. By contrast, the more ornate, Renaissance-influenced styles with ball

and bead turnings on arms, legs, and stretchers were also popular. In addition, red velvet fabric over padding often replaced tooled leather of earlier styles.

Haciendas made extensive use of heavier, more rustic-style utility tables, often with Spanish-influenced splayed legs and box-like enclosed stretchers. In remote locations, simpler styles were developed by local hacienda carpenters. Other later styles included both straight and turned leg examples with *faldones*, or skirts. These tables featured open

Opposite: Green paint has preserved an old tin nicho from Chihuahua. Collection of Bertha Cardenas.

Left: A Saint Francis wood-and-tile nicho was designed by A. Hays Town for Hemisphere Manufacturing. (Durham Trading, Austin, Texas.)

mortise-and-tenon construction and were used commonly in kitchens, workshops, and tack rooms. Altar tables were also prominent, used against walls where pictures of saints and loved ones could accompany a devotional display of flowers, mementos, and candles.

Popular dining-room tables included Spanish-influenced, trestle-style pieces with incised carving on the legs. During the Porfiriato, large and elaborate *comedores*, or dining rooms, prompted the addition of Mexican Chippendale styles or Victorian imports, featuring walnut and mahogany veneers.

Used for storing important documents, inventory books, and valuables, *armarios*, or armoires, featured intricate construction and often ornate carving on front and side panels as well as on the *copete*, or crown. Usually smaller in scale, *roperos*, or wardrobes, were used for storing clothing and often displayed painted floral or country scenes on the front doors.

ACCENTS

The hacienda's decorative accents ranged from the beautiful and unexpected to highly decorative and utilitarian. Mixes of locally made elements and European imports were common. Old charro spurs were hung over baroque sideboards; framed christening gowns and antique firearms were displayed beneath ox-yoke light fixtures. Although the Porfiriato featured extravagant touches, including colorful leaded-glass windows, ornate gas lamps, and wallpaper with English country scenes, the simpler utilitarian elements always had a presence somewhere on the hacienda.

Regardless of the size of the casa grande—modest to monumental—signs of devotion were always present. Crosses of painted wood, iron, and stone were popular in all forms, and they often portrayed the symbols associated with the Crucifixion. Set in courtyards or gardens, stone crosses were often enveloped by hedges or flowering vines. Stone statues were also popular, usually set within wall niches. Altar tables were surrounded by carved-wood patron santos, candlesticks, and candelabras found in every shape and size. The most prized were those turned on a lathe and gessoed, or gold-leafed. Stone-carved angels also took a variety of perches—sometimes standing atop fountains and doors or sitting solo in gardens.

The hacienda had countless locations to display pottery and stone vessels. From patios with fountains and shallow reflecting pools to ponds, rooftop terraces, and formal

Opposite: Large santos appoint a colonial sabino table. Collection of Fred Pottinger.

Above: An antique red armoire with painted flowers sits beneath a painting of Our Lady of Guadalupe in a sunlit colonial patio in Mérida.

gardens, locally made pots and stone feeding troughs were often given double duty as planters. Simple stone sundials were occasionally placed in the main courtyards or near the stable yard. Carved wall niches were also found in entrance halls, under portals, and in grand salons—most often home to carved saints but sometimes a display of ceramics or a blooming plant. In Mérida, Hacienda Cucul's collection of old stone vessels are sprinkled throughout the grounds—surrounding the original limestone water well, sitting atop slim pedestals as planters and topping off the end of the hacienda's aqueduct.

Water-filter stones were used to purify drinking water and were mounted on wooden or iron stands. Water was poured into the conical-shaped hollow stone beneath which a ceramic pot was placed to collect the purified water. At Hacienda San Gabriel de Barrera, the filter stone was placed in a hallway niche and enclosed by wooden spindled gates, allowing light and air to circulate.

Carved-stone and iron elements always add an intriguing flavor to outdoor spaces. A congregation of stone saints watch over Fred Pottinger's interior courtyard.

ARCHITECTURAL ELEMENTS

THE NOVELIST PAYNO VISITED A GREAT HACIENDA IN THE MID-NINETEENTH CENTURY AND LEFT THIS ACCOUNT: *"THE HOUSE OF THE SAUZ HACIENDA WAS IN FACT A FORTIFIED CASTLE. THE FACADE WAS MADE UP OF A HIGH, BROAD ARCHWAY ENDING ON BOTH SIDES IN TWO tall towers with turrets, which were matched by two others guarding the back of the house. The azotea was surrounded by merlons behind which a soldier could keep under cover, so that once the massive oak door reinforced with iron bands was closed, a siege would be necessary to take that building. In the patio, which was large, three or four coaches, each with its own string of eight mules, could have entered, turned around as in a circus, and passed again through the portal, which led to the open country."*

As the haciendas in Mexico were built over a span of four centuries, their architectural styles reflect the style in vogue at the time they were built, along with the technology and building materials available in the region. The eclecticism expressed by the fantasies of the late-nineteenth-century pulque hacienda owners of Hildalgo and the *henequén* hacienda owners of the Yucatán led to neo-Gothic castles being built just pastures apart from French rococo haciendas. These examples give a glimpse of the architectural styles one can encounter when attempting to classify haciendas according to style.

The hacienda's architectural elements—both inside and out—offer a tangible link to the rich heritage of Mexico's traditional construction techniques. Shaped in part by differing climates and indigenous natural resources, regional differences are found in a variety of construction elements. From stone, adobe, and wood to rammed earth and plastering methods, today's architects and builders

Hacienda Yokdzonot's entrance features exposed stone detailing, adding contrast to walls painted with mineral pigment.

find inspiration in hacienda elements and continue to apply them to contemporary houses on both sides of the border. In true Spanish colonial tradition, the arched *portales*, or covered porches, are a favored area of communication between the rooms of the house. They remain one of the most popular architectural details in Mexican-influenced homes today.

Opposite: Hacienda Poxilá's extensive stable and barn area features a tranquil lily pond set against the formal arched gates to the outlying corrals.

Right: A sitting area outside the dining room at Hacienda Cucul, features a recessed painted nicho.

Decorative details also include masonry vaulting techniques, forged ironwork; talavera tile; *rajueleado*, a pre-Hispanic masonry chinking technique; *alfarjes*, or intricate Moorish wooden ceilings; and *tecalli*, a translucent onyx used for windows that has its roots in the pre-Hispanic era.

Massive simplicity was the common denominator of early colonial architecture, and the use of *cantera*, or stone, added great elegance and solidity to the hacienda. In the hand

of Mexican craftsmen, stone is one of the most majestic and enduring building materials. Throughout the centuries, many haciendas were designed with defensive measures, including high perimeter walls and observation towers.

Doors were also crafted in impressive proportions with the addition of large iron *clavos* and strap hinges for extra strength and durability. Today, many surviving examples still retain their vitality and evidence of hearty craftsmanship. The *puerta de carcel*, or jail door, was also common, as each hacienda had its own private jail. The jail door's open lattice pattern is one of the more popular styles being interpreted today as headboards and coffee tables.

The pointed arches seen over corral entrances of cattle haciendas in the Yucatán are technically known as *conoipal* arches. Mistakenly but commonly referred to as Moorish

arches, the origins of them stems from Gothic architecture. A sign of status, the wealth of a hacienda's holdings in cattle was symbolized by grand arches. The most prosperous haciendas boasted double conoipal arches at their entrances.

Marcos, or carved stone frames, usually surrounded doors and windows. They were constructed in a variety of stone depending on the region's local resources (gray volcanic rock in Colima, natural green hues in Oaxaca, rosy pink in Guanajuato, and golden yellow in Zacatecas). Carved stone cornices, moldings, and pilasters were also prevalent. Massive grain-storage buildings were most often constructed in stone and regularly featured *ojo de buey*, or ox-eye windows, in their design. Also prominent on grain-producing haciendas were outdoor stone threshing rings commonly placed in the central courtyard.

Stone aqueducts are tributes to the great masons since many still stand today in majestic form. Constructed on those estates needing field irrigation or power to run processing mills, these aqueducts are impressive monuments to the working world of the

hacienda. Since many are no longer in use, they have been put to new use as dramatic displays for decorative plantings and innovative water gardens. In Morelos, the owners of Hacienda San Gabriel de las Palmas innovatively redirected their aqueduct to create an impressive waterfall in front of their courtyard.

The fancifully carved stone *canales*, or rain spouts, are hollowed-out stone cylinders used to remove rain water from a building. They ideally showcase the Mexican craftsman's talent for turning necessities into objects of beauty. It was customary to shape them in animal forms, such as lions, eagles, serpents, and mythological spirits. Commonly placed on

Opposite and left: At Hacienda Temozón, an old watering tub is now home to lily pads in the former corral. Nearby, a brightly painted courtyard features a grouping of old stone feeding vessels.

Above: A decorative canale, or rain spout, takes the dramatic form of a fanciful serpent.

the street facades of colonial-style buildings to drain roofs, haciendas often featured them in courtyards as well as integrated them into the aqueduct system.

Nichos de concha, or shell niches, were recessed in walls and placed over windows and doorways for decorative focus. Many concha motifs have also been used as architectural accents over beds or dressing tables.

Opposite: The front entrance of Hacienda Yokdzonot reveals a hint of the interior courtyard beyond.

Right: The subterranean space once used for sugar storage at Hacienda San Gabriel de Las Palmas features an impressive vaulted ceiling, which adds drama to its new use as a dining hall.

Bóvedas de cañón, or the art of crafting vaulted ceilings, was taught to local artisans by the Spanish craftsmen in early colonial times. Often left natural with exposed brick, these recessive ceilings are also plastered and painted. This technique is ideally suited for roofing long and narrow spaces and is often seen in large dining and living rooms.

HACIENDA KITCHENS

ONE OF THE MOST CAPTIVATING AND BUSY ROOMS IN THE HACIENDA, THE *COCINA*, OR KITCHEN, ALWAYS BECKONED WITH SIMMERING AROMAS, CONVERSATION, AND A COLORFUL ARRAY OF CERAMIC TILE AND LOCAL CRAFTS. EACH HACIENDA KITCHEN HAD ITS OWN SECRETS, recipes, and delights. Because these kitchens often had to prepare meals for hundreds of people, they were spacious, well equipped, and always humming with activity. They centered around the tiled *brasero*, or hearth, where charcoal-burning stoves were set into long or horseshoe-shaped counters. In addition to the countertops, tile was used throughout — on floors, walls, and sometimes even the ceilings. Early hacienda kitchens were influenced by the cavernous kitchens of the colonial convents. In Puebla, the vaulted-ceiling kitchen of the Convento de Santa Rosa is a masterful example of a space smothered in small glazed tiles. Here, the famed *mole poblano* made its first appearance in Mexican cuisine.

Many haciendas featured two kitchen areas. The main kitchen was used for daily meals and those prepared for fiestas; the other, which included an adobe *horno*, or oven, was dedicated to both bread baking and tortilla making. In the main kitchen, the stove featured large ventilating hoods, often ornamented with fluting or simply decorated with garlands of garlic, local pottery, or sometimes a carved-wood *Cristo*.

Against a backdrop of lustrous tile, hacienda kitchens were simply furnished with hearty wooden prep tables and benches, stools, and chairs for sitting long hours to prepare foods. Always present was the ubiquitous *trastero*, or open cupboard, designed to hold plates and cups within easy reach. Piles of

The Fullerton's newly restored kitchen features a counter fashioned from old English Minton tile. Casa de Máquinas, Yucatán.

parsley, cilantro, and chiles would fill handwoven baskets. Stacks of large clay *ollas*, or cooking pots, were often stacked upside down, awaiting daily use for rice, beans, and moles. Present in every cocina were the three-legged, pre-Hispanic stone *metates* (used to grind corn and chocolate), *bateas*, or dough bowls, earthenware *comales* for cooking tortillas, and copper cauldrons for boiling stews. Iron wall racks would hold a sea of spoons, ladles, and chocolate whisks. Simple, wooden spice racks, sometimes decorated with scalloped edges or chip-carving, were lined with jars of peppercorns, cloves, and cinnamon sticks.

As the haciendas reached their most prosperous era in the eighteenth and nineteenth centuries, many *comedores*, or dining rooms, were enlarged because entertaining in large numbers became more prevalent. By contrast, the kitchens continued their simple streamlined designs; however, meals were prepared in more fanciful ways with dishes served on fine European china and linen-draped tables.

Daily fare on the hacienda was a vivid reflection of the wealth and tastes of the *hacendado*, or hacienda owner, as well as the raw resources available on the hacienda itself. In the north, the cattle hacienda's daily fare focused on meat and dairy dishes. The central region of Morelos and Cuernavaca saw the early cultivation of sugarcane brought to the New World from Cuba by Hernán Cortés. Since sugar was a relatively new and expensive addition to the New World's cuisine, it made its way into the grand hacienda kitchens as a sign of wealth and status. Thus, fiestas and weddings always featured a plethora of sweet stews and desserts.

Mrs. Alec-Tweedie left this account of a hacienda kitchen in the late 1800s: "In the house itself, a number of servants are employed: there is always one, and sometimes there are two servants allotted to each member of the family. Then again one woman is constantly employed making tortillas for the kitchen and the clerks, and she is literally engaged all day in grinding her Indian corn and patting out her cakes."

The early colonial period brought a culinary marriage between the native foods of Mexico and the influences of the Spanish influx. In the convents and hacienda kitchens of Spanish aristocracy, native cooks began to blend the foods of the ancient Aztecs and Mayans—corn, beans, chiles, tomatoes, chocolate, pumpkins, wild turkeys, and ducks, along with the Spanish contribution of wheat, rice, meats, cinnamon, almonds, and citrus fruits. In the early colonial days, bread made from wheat was still a new cuisine and was mostly consumed by Spaniards. As wheat consumption continued to gain wider acceptance,

hacienda kitchens produced more breads and pastries; however, the indigenous population continued to favor corn in all its forms.

Regional hacienda specialties also developed as cooks experimented with the resources in their area. In the state of Coahuila, a pulque hacienda became renowned for its *pulque* bread, made with the fermented alcoholic drink extracted from the hacienda's

maguey plants. The state of Oaxaca, today known as "the land of seven moles," was well known for its complex mole pastes made from the region's chiles, spices, nuts, seeds, chocolate, and dried fruits. Served for generations in a Oaxaca hacienda, the traditional *mole negro*, or black mole, is still made today and offered by the Cabrera family at La Olla, a popular Oaxaca City restaurant.

A hidden interior courtyard displays an impressive stone cross and iron wall sculpture made by Alberto Salum. Yucatán specialties are served beneath a shady 300-year-old rubber tree. Alberto's Continental Patio, Mérida.

New haciendas, such as Hacienda Xixim in the Yucatán, are still employing their land's native harvests for daily culinary preparations. Xixim's chef, Ruben Dario Yam Lara, makes good use of *chaya*, the green leafy vegetable native to the Yucatán, just as his sixteenth-century predecessors did, incorporating it into myriad dishes and sauces and steeping it for tea. The hacienda also continues its centuries-old tradition of harvesting honey from its own bees, making jungle honey for breakfast hotcakes. Even the Mayan tradition of *pollo pibli* is still prepared as it was in colonial times—wrapping the chicken in banana leaves to cook in a covered earthen pit.

RECIPES

ESTOFADO DE BODAS CHICKEN FOR A WEDDING

This recipe is courtesy of Diana Kennedy and Roberto Santibañez. It is a typical wedding stew that was served at hacienda weddings in Oaxaca at the turn of the century. Special thanks to restaurant Fonda San Miguel, Austin, Texas.

Broth
6 large servings of chicken
1/2 small white onion, roughly sliced
3 garlic cloves, peeled
Salt to taste

Sauce
About 6 tablespoons pork lard, vegetable oil, or chicken fat
1 small onion, finely chopped
4 garlic cloves, finely chopped
2 pounds (900 grams) tomatoes, thinly sliced
1/2 cup raisins
1/4 cup slivered almonds
12 pitted green olives, halved
3 whole jalapeño *chiles en escabeche*, quartered
2 tablespoons juice from chiles
1 tablespoon sugar
1 teaspoon dried oregano, crumbled
3 peppercorns
3 cloves
1/4-inch cinnamon stick

Vegetables & Fruit
12 ounces potatoes, peeled and thickly sliced
8 ounces plantain, peeled and sliced lengthwise
2 thick slices pineapple, peeled, cored, and quartered

1. Cover the chicken, onion, and garlic with water; add salt, and bring to a simmer. Continue simmering until the chicken is just tender, about 30 minutes. Set aside to season in the broth while preparing the sauce.

2. Heat 3 tablespoons of lard in a skillet, add the onion and garlic, sprinkle with salt to taste, and fry without browning for about 1 minute. Add the tomatoes and cook over fairly high heat for about 5 minutes. Add the raisins, almonds, olives, chiles, chile juice, sugar, and oregano; continue simmering. Crush or grind spices together and add to pan. Add 2 cups of the broth in which the chicken was cooked and continue cooking for about 5 minutes more.

3. Shortly before serving, heat about 3 tablespoons lard in a skillet and fry the potatoes, covered, turning them over from time to time, until tender and well browned. Drain. In the same fat (add a little more if necessary), add the plantain and fry until well browned. Drain.

4. Ten minutes before serving, add the chicken pieces to the sauce and a little more broth if necessary to dilute it to medium consistency. Add the pineapple and cook over low heat for about 10 minutes. Test for saltiness. Top the dish with the fried potato and plantain and serve.

MOLE NEGRO BLACK MOLE

This recipe is courtesy of the Cabrera family and is served at their Oaxacan restaurant, *La Olla. Mole negro,* or black mole, is a mainstay of Oaxaca's traditional moles used in festivals, such as fandangos, birthdays, and especially Day of the Dead. Its preparation is a ritual that includes the whole family's participation on every level, from its making to its eating. Mole negro is recognized for its strong flavor and its power to unite the family.

3 pieces black *chilhaucle* chiles	1 piece clove
2 pieces Mexican *pasilla* chiles	1 teaspoon oregano
2 pieces *mutato* chiles	1 teaspoon thyme
5 garlic cloves	1 teaspoon *almondoroz*
1 onion	2 slices bread
3 tomatoes	50 grams lard
3 green tomatoes (*tomatillos*)	50 grams chocolate
8 pieces almond	6 pieces of chicken
100 grams raisins	1 1/2 liters chicken broth
100 grams sesame seeds	Salt to taste
1 piece black pepper	50 grams sugar

1. Clean and de-vein all the chiles. Cook the chicken in 2 liters of water for 20 minutes. Cook the tomatoes and green tomatoes in 1/2 liter of water for 15 minutes. Fry the garlic and the onion together. Using a frying pan with 25 grams of lard, fry all the chiles until they are crispy with a cardboard-like texture and set them aside. Next, individually fry the almonds, raisins, sesame seeds, and bread. Later add the oregano, thyme, almondoroz, pepper, and clove.

2. Once the ingredients have been fried, place them all in a blender with 1/2 liter of chicken broth and blend thoroughly. In a large pot (preferably clay) combine the remaining 25 grams of lard and the contents of the blender. Stir the mixture continuously above medium heat for 5 minutes, then add the cooked tomatoes (completely mashed) and the rest of the chicken broth, stirring continuously. Season using the chocolate, sugar, and salt. The texture should be thick. Serve with rice over turkey or chicken.

CALABASITAS RELLENAS STUFFED BABY MAYAN SQUASH

This recipe is courtesy Chef Ruben Dario Yam Lara, Hacienda Xixim, Yucatán. A traditional Mayan dish prepared in Yucatán's hacienda kitchens, *but-bi* uses baby wild squash (*mumun kuun*) that are indigenous to the Yucatán region and available year-round. Traditionally this dish was served for special occasions and was often filled with meat from the *jabali*, or wild pigs, that inhabit the *monte,* or dry jungle, in the Yucatán.

1. Preheat oven 10 minutes at 480 F.

   6 small young squash (*calabasitas*)
 200 grams Oaxaca cheese or Monterey Jack

   Filling
 1/8 pound butter (1/2 stick)
 1/2 pound ground pork (unsmoked leg or shoulder)
 200 grams salami, chopped
  50 grams bacon, chopped
 100 grams *chorizo* (sausage)
   1 sweet bell pepper, finely chopped
   1 carrot, finely chopped
   3 cloves garlic, minced
     Dash pepper
     Dash salt

   Sauce
   8 tablespoon flour
   6 cups water
   2 tablespoon chicken bouillon
   1 teaspoon shortening
 1/4 onion, grilled
 1/4 tomato, grilled
   1 whole Mayan chile (*Xkat Ik*) or sweet bell pepper, grilled

2. Wrap calabasitas in aluminum foil and bake for 20 minutes. Remove from oven and let cool.

3. Prepare filling. Sauté on high heat for 3 minutes until tender: butter, ground pork, salami, bacon, chorizo, bell pepper, carrot, garlic. Add salt, pepper. Remove from heat. Set aside.

4. Remove the aluminum foil from calabasitas and cut a round hole in top of squash. Remove all the pulp. Stuff calabasitas with prepared filling. Set aside.

5. Prepare sauce. In steamer, dissolve flour in water. Add chicken bouillon, shortening, onion, tomato, and chili and cook over medium heat for 5 minutes. Stir constantly until mixture thickens and comes to a boil.

6. Place the calabasitas in steamer and reduce to low heat. Cook 10 minutes longer. Cover the top holes in the calabasitas with cheese.

7. Serve calabasitas in a flat soup bowl covered with sauce.

WORKING HACIENDAS

HACIENDA XIXIM

An arcaded mirador encloses the front portal of Hacienda Xixim in the Yucatán jungle. A locally made cedar table features carved legs with Mayan-inspired glyphs.

Once a sixteenth-century cattle estate, Hacienda Xixim (pronounced Shi—sheem) is hidden in the Mayan-speaking jungles of the Yucatán, surrounded by the remains of ancient lost cities, caves, and *cenotes*, or natural underground wells. When present-day owner Robert Gow found the crumbling estate quite by accident, Xixim had no floor and no roof.

The massive stone *casa principal*, or main house, was filled with hundred-foot-tall trees that had grown from seed after the roof collapsed. Once the removal of jungle over-growth revealed the estate's majestic arcaded facade and original four-foot-thick walls, Gow knew he had found his own private hacienda retreat. But it was his vision for Xixim—one that would be enriching to the land and local community—that really sparked the passionate restoration of the property.

Although the one-time cattle hacienda had subsequently had two reincarnations—one as a thriving *henequén*, or sisal operation, and the latter as a producer of the fiber sansevieria—it was Gow who readied it for its third livelihood: a thriving bamboo hacienda employing Mayan Indians in the creation of garden gates, fences, furniture, accents, and even full-size bamboo structures. This operation's blessings are many—work close to home for the local Indians, rejuvenation of the environment, and, Gow hopes, the development of a replacement crop for henequén, the green gold that brought the region so much wealth during Yucatán's Golden Age, roughly 1840 to 1920.

An American businessman, Gow is also known as an avid environmentalist with a blazing entrepreneurial talent. In addition to building one of North America's largest cattle and poultry enterprises, he has directed international oil and gas operations. In 1969, he began a non-blooming tropical-plant plantation in the jungles of Guatemala, which later became the largest exporter of exotic plants in the world.

With Gow's deep-rooted passion for nature, he made his first priority the grounds, even though Xixim's house needed much attention. Orange, pink grapefruit, lime, sour orange, lemon, and tangerine trees were planted and now bear prolifically. Gow also designed a dramatic entrance to the hacienda; flame trees now surge in pairs along the long drive, creating a blaze of red in late summer. In 1995, the first iron bamboo seeds were

70

planted in small plastic bags filled with bagasse left over from nineteenth-century henequén operations. Not surprisingly, his concentrated digging and planting efforts also afforded him rich decorative discoveries.

In addition to uncovering Xixim's original entrance arch on the east side of the property, Gow unearthed a large carved-stone shell buried in many feet of soil. Because *Xixim* translates to "shell" in Mayan, this find has since obtained a position of honor on the estate, poised in a wall niche atop the front entrance's commanding stairwell. Set adjacent to a decorative bamboo-brush column, the stone shell serves as a marquee to the hacienda's newfound role.

Restoration began in 1986. The project was adapted as much as possible to the building's original layout in an attempt to preserve and recover its special features and stone-chinked walls. Plumbing elements were integrated and local materials were used to enhance the building's original look and value.

The site was first cleared of all rubble and debris; then the original fifteen-foot walls were surveyed and probed to brace where necessary. Unstable elements were removed, door wells were reinforced with concrete slabs, and exterior walls were rebuilt with local stone. Specially designed tiles commissioned in Puebla were used to line the kitchen and bathrooms. Although the fifteen-foot-high ceilings are now of steel-reinforced concrete, they are covered with *vigas*, or beams, cut from the native trees of the hacienda.

Xixim's original casa principal was built upon an 8/10-acre platform. This platform, about fifteen feet high, was erected by building stone and concrete walls and by layering the space within the walls with dirt. From the platform, three *norias*, or wells, were dug into the underground aquifer. The hacienda's water was stored in a giant, round, stone-buttressed tank on this earthen platform. From this tank, aqueducts were built to irrigate four *hectares* (about eight acres) of fruit, vegetable, and flower gardens.

Many months were spent cleaning out the hacienda's norias that had been silted up over time. Originally constructed by the Spanish, these square wells were operated with a belt-and-bucket system driven by a gearing arrangement powered by mules. Before the norias, Mayans collected rainwater in underground cisterns called *chultunes*, or they descended on foot by stairs and ladders into underground cenotes to collect water in gourds or pottery jars. Today, Xixim's norias are in use with submersible electric pumps. The original water tank obstructed the view from the back portal and, thus, was decimated with dynamite to make room for a more visually pleasing swimming pool. Added to the

Opposite: A former sixteenth-century cattle estate, Hacienda Xixim was restored to its former splendor by owner Robert Gow.

Above: A decorative brush column is made from bamboo harvested at Hacienda Xixim.

Opposite: Pictured is a close-up view of Hacienda Xixim's Ticul bamboo fence panel.

Below, left: Running between Xixim's bamboo groves, the original rock-bed path was once connected to a narrow-gauge rail system powered by mules that allowed the henequén, or sisal, fibers to be transported to the fábrica, or factory house.

Below, top right: A pile of freshly cut bamboo awaits assembly into custom garden gates.

Bottom right: Local Mayan crafts-men assemble bamboo gates with wrapped vines.

backyard was a layer of *suelo rojo*, the local rich soil, upon which single sprigs of St. Augustine grass were planted. Today a plush lawn surrounds the pool.

Well-suited to the tropical climate, the hacienda's open plan encourages outdoor living among its many outdoor rooms: the arcaded terrace, patios, and back portal. Surrounded by lush vegetation and crimson bougainvillea, the front terrace offers a sweeping view of the entrance and is the heart of the home, the essential daily gathering spot for meals and conversation.

Dinners are served by candlelight, and friends and family gather around a large cedar table that comfortably seats twelve. Crafted by a local artisan, the table's hearty legs feature hand-carved Mayan glyphs. For variety, dinners are often served in the hacienda's former schoolhouse located across the yard on the north side of the pool. Its eighteen-foot ceiling and stark walls offer a dramatic setting. A large window overlooks the old growing fields to a small hill beyond. When Gow's bamboo is more mature, he hopes to build a unique bamboo house on this hill and connect it to the platform of the casa principal by a bamboo suspension bridge.

Throughout the main house, ample doorways allow cross-ventilation and connect the outdoor rooms to the library and kitchen, allowing the rooms to flow into each other. The master bedroom and two additional bedrooms are tucked away behind antique doors at one end of the platform level of the main house. One, converted from the hacienda's *calabozo*, or private jail, used to hold peóns in need of punishment. Bedroom interiors are accented by bamboo headboards and eight-foot-high windows affording a compelling view of the jungle. Scattered throughout the main house, comfortable wicker chairs encourage reading and frequent siestas. Xixim's stark yet elegant interiors pay homage to the rich architectural details. Here, the luxuriant stone textures are the artful focus.

In addition to the removal of the water tank, a tunnel was excavated to connect the first and second floors with an iron spiral staircase. Adjacent to the main entrance, a large stone fish pond was constructed for raising *talapia* fish, whose presence helps minimize the mosquito population.

As with many haciendas, Xixim is a world unto itself. Even today, it is self-sufficient. Fruits are grown in the hacienda's orchards, fresh fish are caught right outside the kitchen, and honey is harvested from the hacienda's very own bee population.

Originally constructed by the Mayans, rock roadbeds were also discovered on the property. During the henequén boom, narrow-gauge rail lines were laid along these roadbeds and mule-driven carts traveled along these rails, transporting henequén leaves from field to *fabrica*, or factory. Today, these well-built roadbeds make an extensive network of jungle hiking trails throughout the property.

From his private world in the Mexican jungle, Gow's innovative efforts with Hacienda Xixim are having a strong impact on the United States home-design and garden markets. As a result, Gow has received a number of patents, and he and his partner, David Flanagan, have additional patents pending.

The Yucatán bamboo designs, including fences, gates, and furniture, are shipped quickly and easily from the Port of Progreso to New Orleans in a matter of a few days. Designers from Long Island to California have discovered how easily the natural bamboo elements mix into a variety of design themes. Most recently, methods have been developed to dye bamboo various colors, allowing even greater design diversity. The craftsmen at Hacienda Xixim continue to develop innovative techniques to present this versatile material in new ways. Additionally, the wide-ranging benefits of bamboo as a building material—its strength and resistance to humidity—have also captured the attention of architects and designers worldwide.

The thick stone corral walls at Hacienda Oxtapacab no longer contain cattle; instead, they protect rows and rows of potted and numbered coconut palm hybrids. Adding a graceful touch to the scene is a majestic *piich* tree that presides over this eco-friendly project operated by Colatinco Enterprises in the Yucatán.

Owner Rafael Aristi found Oxtapacab's casa principal and extensive grounds to be ideal for housing the certified coconut palm plantation, also known as Huerta Madre, or mother plantation, of the Malayan dwarf. Together with partners Josefina Larrain and Paul Fullerton, Aristi's plantation produces pure Malayan dwarfs that serve as mothers in the creation of *maypan* hybrids. The maypan's remarkable quality is that it is almost immune to the lethal yellowing disease that has devastated the Pacific Tall varieties along the Caribbean coast and Florida.

Built in the early nineteenth century, Oxtapacab's stately white facade is ornamented by an elegant veranda supported by fluted columns and a decorative balustrade. Following its days as a cattle hacienda, Oxtapacab cultivated henequén in the early twentieth century and was most recently converted by Aristi to its present-day role. The massive blue-speckled stairwell is flanked by a pair of stone statues depicting workers carrying henequén bundles on their backs.

Inside, the casa principal houses offices that overlook the central corrals and a variety of lush planting areas, outbuildings, and arched gates. Stone steps at the rear of the house lead to myriad shaded areas where hundreds of coconuts line up next to a maze of stone aqueduct channels. Here, the grounds of an old hacienda are sprouting with life once again. Oxtapacab's new role has tremendous benefits because Colatinco Enterprises provides certified material to a variety of regions, from Mexico's Veracruz and Guerrero to the Caribbean and beyond. This special agricultural effort allows many other countries, many of which have yet to experience the devastating effects of lethal yellowing, to prepare in advance, establishing a source for hearty resistant palms that can ultimately reverse the economic and ecological damage caused by the disease.

Opposite: The thick stone walls at Hacienda Oxtapacab no longer contain cattle. Instead they protect rows and rows of potted coconut palm hybrids.

Above: Coconuts lie in front of the hacienda's old aqueduct channel.

Opposite: The stairwell is anchored with a statue of a hacienda worker carrying a henequén bundle.

Left, top: The blue-speckled entrance stairs show centuries of wear.

Bottom: Hacienda Oxtapacab's former water-holding tank is now a swimming pool.

HACIENDA MÉNDEZ LEÓN

Not far from the ruins of Mitla where the Zapotecs settled in 600 B.C., an old working hacienda stands testament to the region's growth in mezcal cultivation and production and one family's commitment to centuries of tradition. Inside and out, Hacienda Méndez León is rich in references to the mezcal legacy started in 1750 by family patriarch, Lic. Guadalupe Méndez.

Still in the hands of the founding family, Lic. Juan José Méndez León Garcia has updated the eighteenth-century hacienda into a comfortable home and working environment. Here, day-to-day business details are overseen by family members—from cultivation of the mezcal fields to marketing and shipping. The expanded mezcal operation is located at a nearby work yard and distillery.

Mezcal was the drink of the noble Zapotec monarchs. It was not until the Spaniards arrived in Oaxacan territory that its consumption was generalized. The time-honored traditions restricting its use to Indian ceremonies have given way to a widespread popularity that now sees mezcal bottles distributed internationally to France and Asia. Restaurants in the American Southwest have also started sharing mezcal's engaging flavors by importing Oaxacan mezcal on a regular basis.

Mezcal's exotic flavor comes from its complex production process. To release their juices, the hearts of the agave plants are placed in ditches with torch pine, firewood, volcanic rock, and dry grass. After three days of roasting, the product is removed and taken to an area where the bagasse is ground with a heavy millstone powered by a horse. Then it is fermented in vats and stored in huge copper distillation apparatuses.

Echoing the vital role the family hacienda has played in the business, their Mezcal Legendario de Oaxaca brand features a signature bottle label with the hacienda's exterior. The impressive adobe facade fronts a cobblestone street and reveals its Baroque influences.

Upon entering the grand entrance hall, one is reminded of the family's fascinating heritage. Painted on the wall is a faux scrolled document, chronicling the names and dates of each generation of owners. Close by, an old-fashioned wall-mounted telephone stands over a hearty slab bench. The entrance leads to a flower-filled stone courtyard alive with bougainvillea, birds, and music from the adjacent church. Shady portals surround all four sides of the courtyard and open into the main rooms of the house. Old oxen yokes are newly hung as light fixtures, simple sconces dot the stone columns, and agave paintings by local Oaxacan artists enliven the walls.

The stone entrance of the Méndez León hacienda leads to a flower-filled interior courtyard.

82

Opposite: A whimsical virtuosity in green Oaxacan stone, the corner design of the Méndez León hacienda reveals its baroque influence. The corner pediment that crowns the parapet walls features ascending carved volutes, forming an arched niche that once held the saint who protected the mezcal enterprise. A base was added to protect the corner from damage caused by wagon wheels hitting the corner when attempting to turn, a regional response to a very real problem of an earlier era.

Right: Antique typewriters used by the hacienda's past generations rest easily on a table made out of a door found on the estate. The base features a mixed-utilitarian past: an old safe and wheel hubs.

Eighteen-foot ceilings infuse the rooms with elegance, and family heirlooms and antiques lend an air of romance. Antique typewriters used by past generations rest easily on a table made from a massive old door from the estate. The base is a secure mix of the hacienda's past—an old safe and wagon-wheel hubs. A collection of antique firearms are displayed, and a nearby player piano fills the salon with classic Mozart. Many of the bedrooms feature recently added skylights and period furnishings, including headboards painted with idyllic country scenes.

Opposite: Rows of agaves surround the Méndez León mezcal hacienda.

Above: An early step in the mezcal-making process, agave hearts have been prepared for baking in an earthen pit. Mezcal is derived from the Nahuatl word mexcalmetl, meaning agave species. Over 120 species of agaves have been recorded in the Americas from which alcoholic drinks: tequila, mezcal, and pulque, are made. Mezcal, known for its complex, smoky flavor, can be distilled from one of several species of "magueys mescaleros," or mezcal-producing magueys, but tequila is made from only one species of agave, agave tequilana, the blue agave.

ARTISTS' HACIENDAS

PAUL FULLERTON AND JOSEFINA LARRAIN

Aluminum sculpture by artist Paul Fullerton stands in a hallway under an iron transom original to the casa de máquinas.

Tucked away on the lush grounds of Hacienda Sacchich are three limestone buildings and an eighty-foot chimney tower that were once the heart of this estate's henequén-processing operation. Discovering the deserted structures eight years ago while traveling across the Yucatán, artists Paul Fullerton and Josefina Larrain moved from New York to creatively transform the *casa de máquinas,* or machine house, into an artful contemporary residence.

Surrounding a palm-filled courtyard, the U-shaped casa de máquinas consists of three rectangular structures that date to the mid-nineteenth century. Inside the former engine house, stark walls sweep upward twenty-two feet to reveal evidence of its previous utilitarian life—iron wheels and massive beams, once part of the steam-driven power plant's intricate system of belts and wheels that used to transfer power throughout the complex. Today, it's hard to imagine the whitewashed rooms of this new home once filled with tons of dilapidated machinery and decades of grease and dirt

Opposite the newly renovated residence stands the building formerly used for baling henequén fibers. It is now a light-filled art studio, thanks to the addition of a nine-foot-wide skylight. Connecting the two buildings is a raised open-air structure that once supported the *desfibradora,* or fiber-extracting machine, that processed the estate's henequén stalks. Below the platform, small rail cars caught the extracted fibers and transported them to nearby drying fields. Today, the partially restored building provides an elevated view of the great lawn, creating a tranquil spot for Fullerton and Larrain to relax with friends.

Since trees and vegetation had taken hold of the interiors, restoration efforts began with roof repairs and overall cleanup. These efforts bore their own fruit. Doors located underneath machinery were rescued from caked layers of grease. A single surviving window shutter was duplicated by a local carpenter to complete the present-day kitchen's authentic details. Throughout the restoration period, Fullerton and Larrain traveled to and from the United States and moved in permanently four years after they began work on the property.

Today, restoration projects continue, as Fullerton and Larrain plan to repair the parapets on all three buildings and replace other original details. The former water storage tank, located behind the casa de máquinas, is now surrounded by newly planted coconut palms and refreshed with a coat of colored cement to create an inviting swimming pool.

Opposite: An old quilt is the highlight of the master bedroom, which also includes twenty-two-foot ceilings and mosquito netting. No effort has been made to conceal the iron wheels affixed to the walls, originally part of a complex belt system in the first machine shop.

Right: The newly restored casa de máquinas, or machine house, features a large airy living room with exposed beams. The cyanotype, entitled Scull Electopithicus, is by Paul Fullerton.

Following pages, left: The hacienda's original water tank that fed the maze of aqueducts has been given a new coat of colored cement for a more relaxed new use.

Opposite: The eighty-foot chimney tower rises above the casa de máquinas compound, providing a constant reminder of the building's utilitarian past. The door surround sports a new coat of red paint to call attention to the colonial doors.

Throughout the main house, furnishings are kept to a minimum with architectural details and art doing most of the decorating. Collections of objects as diverse as pottery shards and sea-fan mobiles are mixed with richly hued textiles, giving the house a cosmopolitan, cultural charm.

The simplicity of the space creates a perfect backdrop for display of Fullerton and Larrain's solar prints and sculptures. A large-scale cyanotype, entitled *Scull Electopithicus*, was created by Fullerton on New Year's Day in 1980, from a sculpture titled *homage a l'inwenteure*. Captivating the eye in the main living area, its presence anchors the large space.

At the north end of the living room is the present-day kitchen, once home to the massive steam engine. High windows allow light to flood warmth into the sunflower-colored room. A long tiled counter presents a surface with a story—an intriguing tie to the original hacienda.

When restoration on the machine house began, Larrain discovered a box of old English Minton tile buried in the ground outside the engine house. Obviously discarded from the hacienda's casa grande, the box of used tiles were leftover halves. Pairing them in a diagonally cut mosaic, Larrain and Fullerton designed their kitchen's *meseta*, or counter, reminiscent of their favorite old counter in the kitchen at Mérida's Casa de Huespedes.

The couple's interest in natural materials and local techniques further directed the progress of the house's restoration. Walls were plastered using the centuries-old method of lime plaster mixed with *baba de nopal*, or cactus juice. Floors were warmed up with the addition of colored cement; sienna tones graced the living room and red-oxide was added to kitchen floors for contrast. Local artisans assisted them in restoring salvaged doors, two of which were acquired from an old bakery and a nearby bus station. New cedar frames were made to surround the door's interior panels. Stripped to a natural state and now hanging in the bedroom, the bus-station doors open to a view of the palm-framed swimming pool.

Fullerton and Larrain have a great interest in palms and are partners in Colatinco Enterprises, a certified coconut palm plantation started by their good friend Rafael Aristi. The plantation produces hybrids immune against lethal yellowing disease and is housed on a nearby hacienda.

SERGIO HERNÁNDEZ

Dramatic contrast of traditional materials play up the structural geometry of artist Sergio Hernández's urban hacienda and reveal the artful eye behind its restoration and design. A stark Japanese lantern illuminates the rich textures of the living room's exposed adobe walls, which also double as an intriguing canvas for a modern graphic display of old polished lock plates. "The rigid unity of materials makes it a house that needs very little decoration," states Hernández. Throughout the newly restored home, variations of space and light create a wide range of atmospheres, providing an intriguing showcase for his artworks and unique collections.

From an early age, Sergio Hernández's life has been surrounded by a world of striking contrasts. This theme and the spirit of fantasy—formed in a place between imagination and a dream—are alive in his paintings and ceramic works. Born in Xochistlapilco, a village in the Mixteca Mountains by the Oaxaca-Puebla border, he began his life in the country but soon migrated with his family to the suburbs of Mexico City. The transition from the lush countryside and its organic forms to the harsh city life with its rush of imagery left a lasting impression on the young eight-year-old. Trained at the Universidad Nacional Autónoma de Mexico and the Instituto Nacional de Bellas Artes in Mexico City, he has become one of Oaxaca's most internationally acclaimed and celebrated artists. His work has been widely exhibited throughout Mexico, Europe, Latin America, and the United States.

Hernández's choice of materials and accents display his love of natural elements. Clay tiles provide a cool surface underfoot; a hand-woven *petate*, or floor mat, adds traditional pattern; massive stone columns add strength to the open-air patio; simple yet elegant tables, chairs, and benches, handcrafted by his brother in *sabino*, or Mexican cypress, add clean lines to the downstairs courtyard that opens into the dining room and living area. Here family and friends gather around the large square table for meals and conversation.

Throughout the home, the variations of space and light create a range of atmospheres, allowing the house to have an abundance of character. One of his favorite areas of the house is the downstairs stone courtyard that faces the pared-down dining room and living area.

Even accents are arranged deliberately to offer textural contrasts. The entrance hall spotlights a collection of hand-carved wood Mexican dance masks, at home against earthy adobe walls. Other objects are purposely packed with surprise: a collection of rare

Opposite: A contemporary Japanese paper lantern illuminates and highlights the textures of an ancient adobe wall. Contemporary dining table and chairs are made from local sabino *at the home of Sergio Hernández, Oaxaca.*

insects—tarantulas, beetles, and praying mantis—sit motionless under glass in his second-floor studio office.

Hernández purchased the deserted and decayed colonial property four years ago and worked together with architects Ramon Torres and Hector Velazquez G. to incorporate the property's existing elements—stone columns and stairways—into their plans. They also designed new elements into the structure to strike a contemporary chord. Large circular win-

Opposite: A collection of rare and exotic insects—beetles, butterflies, and praying mantis—create a contemporary graphic in the second-floor study of the Hernández home in Oaxaca.

Right: Modern furniture sets the mood for the contemporary living room and private courtyard of the Hernández home. The high-walled garden features a reflecting pool and indigenous plants.

Following pages, left: A dramatic welcome, Sergio Hernández's painting on tile graces his entrance foyer. A stone column beckons visitors to enter the courtyard and living area.

Opposite: A coffee table and bench were made in local sabino by the artist's brother. Puppets adorn the wall, and a traditional woven petate from Ocotlán adds intimacy to the area.

dows were added to bring light from the courtyard into second-floor rooms. A spiral stairwell was installed to conveniently connect the master bedroom and study to the heart of the home—the downstairs courtyard and open-air dining room. A second exposed stairway was built to connect the upstairs studio to a newly designed rooftop cactus garden. Placed amidst potted plants, a group of old sugar molds offers geometric visual interest, while *bateas*, or dough bowls, are kept handy for entertaining.

LUIS ZÁRATE

Not far from the city of Oaxaca, a small village clings to a lush hillside abloom with mimosa trees and bougainvillea. Off the main road, a well-worn trail leads to a huge adobe wall distinguished by two enormous millstones set close to its corner. Behind the wall, renowned artist Luis Zárate has metamorphosed a former wheat hacienda and working *molino*, or mill, into a resplendent country home.

The hacienda was built in 1830, and only the walls were left standing when Zárate purchased the property eight years ago. Together with architects Claudina López Morales and Luis Cabral Pérez, Zárate began the two-year restoration effort with a team of talented Oaxacan artisans.

First, roofs were added to keep the structure from continuing deterioration. Rooms piled with dirt were excavated. Plans were drawn up for the addition of circular windows, iron grilles, and balcony railings. Stone surrounds for doors and windows were ordered from the nearby quarry. A welcoming color was chosen for the facade, and red rust, or oxide, was mixed with lye to make the bright pink pigment. Thanks to the effect of the sun, the color soon gave way to a Pompeiian pink, but Zárate aptly calls it "plain pink."

A Oaxacan native, Zárate was born in Tlaxiaco and traveled to Paris to study at the Ecole des Artes Decoratif. His work has been exhibited worldwide, including Spain, Germany, France, Peru, and the United States. Oaxaca proudly claims him as one of its most renowned contemporary artists.

In addition to being an internationally acclaimed painter, Zárate's artistic talents extend to landscape design as well. Along with a group of prominent Oaxacan artists and architects, Zárate designed the impressive Ethno-Botanical Garden of the Ex-Convento de Santo Domingo in Oaxaca City. Zárate's own garden evidences his skill in landscape design as well. Entered through the walled compound's rustic mesquite doors, a multilevel garden beckons with exotic succulents, cacti, and fruit trees. The central garden terrace features a massive *zompantle* tree that provides shade for the main house and is home to the long entangled vines of the *copa de oro* (cup of gold).

At the top of the garden, the present-day swimming pool once operated as the holding tank from which water was channeled downward through stone tunnels to power the hacienda's wheat mill. A moveable gate acted as the tank's valve. Today, these tunnels are accessible from inside the house and have become the ideal wine cellar.

The entrance hall is a tribute to fine craftsmanship at Luis Zárate's home in Oaxaca.

Opposite, top row: This spacious shower includes a garden view. Millstones decorate the garden wall and recall the building's original life as a wheat-mill hacienda.

Bottom: Luis Zárate's painting studio displays a new work, Grasshopper Scribes.

Right: A zompantle tree paints a daily shadow on the entrance to the Zárate hacienda.

RODOLFO MORALES

In his native village of Ocotlán, Oaxaca, world-renowned artist Rodolfo Morales has created a magical artistic haven and has opened his arms wide to touch the people of his community and neighboring pueblos. An ex-soap hacienda—now his garden-filled home and studio—was revived to include spaces for a computer lab, library, and open-air theater for local youths. A cultural center fused with creativity and learning, Morales's home is dedicated to the spirit of the community.

In 1990, the artist established the Rodolfo Morales Cultural Foundation, which focuses on the rescue and restoration of Oaxaca's rich colonial architecture and traditional arts. His noble efforts and projects have made a profound mark on Oaxaca. Most recently, Morales's preservation efforts have included an old colonial home in downtown Oaxaca that he has converted into a charming hotel, resplendent with his signature colorful paintings and old-world antiques.

Standing only a block from the charming Ocotlán plaza and Ex-Convento de Santo Domingo de Guzman, the courtyard entrance of Morales's home is glimpsed from the street through tall wrought-iron gates. The sun-drenched space is bursting with bougainvillea, parrots, and animals, and long corridors and stairwells lead to tucked-away patios and terraces. On the first floor, all the rooms surround the arcaded courtyard that opens to the sun and breezes, and doors are often left open.

Throughout the home, rooms are decorated in a mix of Victorian antiques, native crafts, and spectacular works of stained glass. A parlor room off one bedroom houses Morales's fascinating collection of Mexican toys and folk art gathered from pueblos throughout Mexico. Here and there, he has sprinkled corners with brightly painted ceramics, miniature antique perfume bottles, *santos*, and *retablos*.

The formal dining room is alive with a changing palette of light, thanks to a profusion of brightly colored stained-glass windows. Morales's fondness for stained glass is evident throughout the home as it brightens stairwell windows and culminates in a spectacular second-floor open-air atrium that looks out to the rising mountains beyond Ocotlán.

The back of the house features a large outdoor area, constructed into a mini-theater with the addition of wide terraced steps for audience seating and a staging area for performances. Roaming peacocks enjoy the plant-filled courtyard when it's not in use.

A second-story atrium, sheltered by a stained-glass canopy, overlooks the beautiful Ocotlán valley. Opening onto this large mirador are myriad creative spaces: the artist's painting studio and collage studio, as well as a computer room used by local youths.

Right: Rodolfo Morales paints early in the morning in his light-filled studio in Ocotlán, Oaxaca.

Following page, left: A fanciful Rodolfo Morales painting features a display of chairs in a dramatic real-life extension of the living-room furniture at his newly restored colonial hotel in Oaxaca City.

Following page, right: Chairs painted in fiesta colors are the focal point of this serene courtyard.

RESIDENTIAL HACIENDAS

HACIENDA SANTO DOMINGO DE YUNCU

A private hacienda in the Yucatán features a long portal strung with a sea of hammocks awaiting an afternoon siesta with its tranquil tropical setting of orchids, palms, and citrus trees.

Mayan village tradition and ancient history are alive at Santo Domingo de Yuncu, where architectural and landscape designer Ruth McMurtry resides in the Yucatán *monte*. The hacienda's original chapel is still used by local Mayan villagers, whose voices fill the air with song throughout the year.

In 1996, Santo Domingo de Yuncu was found in an overgrown state yet habitable with minor repairs. Originally built as a cattle hacienda in the seventeenth century, the hacienda was one of many owned by the prominent Peón family. The estate presently consists of the traditional *casa principal*, *capilla*, or chapel, *noria*, or well, pool and tall aqueducts, corrals, and a *taller*, or workshop. A factory to support the work of the late-nineteenth-century henequén boom—constructed to match the existing main house—lies in wait for a new life.

The main well of the hacienda was formed by the progressive erosion of deep rock formations of the ancient Chicxculub crater. A *cenote*, or underground well, ironically rests under the present-day swimming pool.

McMurtry's intrigue with the region was piqued when she visited an abandoned hacienda fifteen years ago. Combining her interests in horticulture, architecture, and indigenous Mayan culture, McMurtry has found that Santo Domingo de Yuncu has been an ideal base for student groups studying a vast range of topics. "The opportunity to apply my theoretical work of cross-cultural, sustainable design strategies to a variety of real situations in such a rich setting has been a unique privilege," McMurtry states.

As an example, to accommodate student guests, bathrooms were installed in the tower building adjacent to the south *pórtico*. An open-sky shower/dressing room features recovered *tejas*, or tiles, which originated in France and traveled to Mexico as ship ballast. "All the construction work is done with the help of the people in the village, all of us learning as we go," adds McMurtry. Adding a modern touch to the exterior, the village tattoo artist—with input from his neighbors—was enlisted to paint an artful abstract design on the facade.

Throughout the hacienda, decorative details and furnishings—both locally made and recycled from hacienda elements—possess their own fascinating tie to local history. A

charming side table on the pórtico is made from one-half of a metal power wheel from the factory. The tabletop is made of *ticul* stone, the local peach-colored marble.

A large door with many layers of peeling paint now serves as a dining table with the addition of a glass top leveled by hose washers. The two pyramid-shaped wooden bases were originally used to form the concrete foundations of irrigation guns. The planks of the forms first served as bee boxes.

Once covered in coral vines and debris, Santo Domingo de Yuncu's grounds provide an ambitious, ongoing challenge. Today, the gardens and orchards are thriving with native plants and experimental plantings introduced by McMurtry. Below the pool, hidden walk-

Opposite: Hacienda Santo Domingo de Yuncu's dining room features a glass-topped table made from an old door originally found in a storeroom on the property.

Above: Native freshwater fish and aquatic plants are raised in the old stone reservoir that once supplied water for the cattle.

ways lead to circles of bamboo and shady corners blooming with native orchids. Beyond the *ceiba*, the sacred tree of the Maya, (also known as Kapok), are sweet-smelling papaya and avocado trees. The estate also inherited four huge laurel trees from India, originally brought to the Yucatán to provide year-round shade for cattle. Today, in the large stone reservoir that supplied water for the cattle in the main corral, McMurtry raises native freshwater fish and a variety of aquatic plants.

"We strive to be good neighbors, promote education, provide employment when feasible, and, overall, to be good land stewards. It is exciting to connect what has gone before to the future," says McMurtry.

The veranda at Hacienda Yokdzonot provides ample room for informal dining. Old stone feeding vessels found on the property add texture to a nearby ledge.

The crumbling overgrown stable at Hacienda Yokdzonot casts a mesmerizing spell on Christopher Holder and Margaret Andrews, working its way into their wedding plans and eventually their daily life. The couple happened upon the deserted fourteen-acre estate outside of Mérida and were swept up in its physical grandeur and intriguing past. The *casa grande*, or main house, had been boarded up for years, but there was no question where restoration would begin—the stable. Both passionate equestrians, they set out to restore the stable building in 1989. One year later, it became their idyllic wedding location. Today, it continues to be a favorite spot for dining and entertaining guests.

Both born in Mexico of United States and Mexican parents, Holder and Andrews have a special affinity for Mexico's rich history and its cultural arts. Andrews is a documentary film producer who has created numerous projects for CNN, PBS, and the BBC. Most recently, she contributed a special segment on Mexico to the *Millennium* series for CNN. Holder, a businessman with diverse holdings in Mexico and the Unites States, has offices in nearby Mérida.

Yokdzonot, Mayan for "house over a *cenote*," was built in the early 1800s. Defining its name, the main house is built over a natural underground well. Because of the intense Yucatán heat, rooms were designed with twenty-foot-high ceilings to effectively keep them cool. Although many haciendas featured elaborate stenciling on these grand-scale walls, Holder and Andrews took a simplified approach to the home's two grand interior rooms. By painting large vertical "frames" of color, they could add drama to the rooms and still allow space for paintings. These same walls continue to hint at the room's former function as sleeping quarters because the hooks once used to support strung-up hammocks for sleeping are still visible.

Not all haciendas have period furnishings collecting dust behind boarded-up windows. Most, however, have architectural elements still intact. Serendipitously, Yokdzonot had both. Delighted to discover a few pieces of antique furniture, including a fourteen-foot mahogany table in the parlor, Holder and Andrews also found two Rufino Tamayo paintings thumbtacked to a library wall.

Covered with layers of celery-green paint, the table required months of stripping to reveal its mahogany grain. A favorite color of a previous *hacendado*, or hacienda owner,

this same celery-colored paint dressed up a few rocking chairs that had also fallen prey to the paintbrush. As local lore had indicated, the previous owner had a penchant for collecting unusual objects, evidenced by a four-foot ceramic Buddha and life-size Snow White—

Opposite: Boasting the luxury of space, strong vertical color stripes sweep the dining-room walls at Hacienda Yokdzonot. The fourteen-foot dining table—originally painted celery green—was discovered in the parlor of the deserted house.

Right: An ancient stone vessel makes a simple statement in its new use as a bathroom sink at Hacienda Yokdzonot.

Preceding page: The elegant stable arcade at Hacienda Yokdzonot graces the entire length of the newly restored building.

accompanied by her seven dwarfs—found standing next to the mahogany table. Unearthed in the stables were more discoveries, including an old horseshoe and a few pre-Hispanic carved stone vessels, one of which now serves as an elegantly simple bathroom sink.

Standing to the west of the main house and nestled amidst large trees are the stables—to the east, the guest house. Requiring major reconstruction, the stables were designed in the hacienda style with the addition of an impressive arcade extending the length of the stables. An identical five-arched facade also graces the nearby guest house. The stable arcade, in addition to providing a shady staging area, doubles as a relaxed setting for conversation and casual meals. To personalize the new buildings, Holder and Andrews added stone-carved family coats of arms to the facades. Inspired by Mérida's profusion of colonial iron window grilles, the couple designed their own decorative grilles for the horse stalls, intertwining their signature initials—H & A—on the handsomely crafted doors.

Opposite: Bearing the initials of Hacienda Yokdzonot's owners, decorative wrought iron grilles adorn the stables.

Right: The jump at Hacienda Yokdzonot replaces traditional hay with henequén fibers. Owner Christopher Holder rides Olympic hopeful A. Beulgari.

Yokdzonot is home to twenty magnificent horses: ten are broodmares and the others are in training and used for show jumping. Their most illustrious horse is A. Beulgari, the son of Abdulla, who won second place in the Los Angeles Olympics. The property features two riding rings; one is a large grass ring that sports many jumps, including the *henequén* jump. Each of the eight corrals includes adjacent small thatched houses that had once served as the original hacienda's workers' quarters. Today they are home to Yokdzonot's prized horses.

One of the outstanding features of Yokdzonot is the tower. As yet unfinished, this edifice is twelve meters high and consists of a four-meter entrance to a twin-story library with a winding staircase up to the reading room. The tower was built especially for Andrew's aunt, who hopes to retire at Yokdzonot and read in the seclusion of her tower.

RESORT HACIENDAS

A POTENT SYMBOL OF RESPITE AND ESCAPE, HACIENDAS ARE IDEALLY SUITED TO BECOME HOTELS AS THEIR VAST LANDS AND UNIQUE COMPLEX OF CORRALS, STABLES, AND OUTBUILDINGS LEND THEMSELVES TO INNOVATIVE DEVELOPMENT. OLD WATER STORAGE TANKS, once a part of intricate irrigation systems, have been easily adapted to impressive pools. Some extend out from old steam-engine rooms and spotlight original machinery as modern-day sculpture. Others take their design cue from the hacienda's state of ruin, as with the sixteenth-century Hotel Hacienda Cortés in Cuernavaca, which features an inviting pool built around old stone support columns.

Throughout the old mining and sugar haciendas, massive stone aqueducts with their awe-inspiring arches are now overgrown with luxuriant vines and exotic plantings and serve as highlights to many hacienda-hotel gardens. San Miguel de Regla in Hidalgo is one of the finest examples, offering nature trails along canals and springs. In Querétaro, Hacienda Galindo has made elegant use of its stone storehouses, turning them into grand ballrooms.

Some haciendas featured mule-driven trolley systems to transport the harvest—sugarcane or *henequén* (sisal) leaves—from fields to factory. Today, guests can literally be transported back to the hacienda era by riding these original flatbed cars along narrow-gauge rail lines through extensive fields and past *cenotes*, or underground caves. In San Luis Potosí, visitors can also take a dip in the same thermal waters that soothed eighteenth-century visitors at Hacienda Gogorrán. In Aguascalientes, Hacienda Ojo Caliente also offers natural springs and tranquil rooms preserved with original Victorian furnishings.

Hacienda Temozón's glowing pool beckons at twilight in front of the estate's nineteenth-century henequén fábrica, or factory.

HACIENDA TEMOZÓN In addition to their inviting country settings, haciendas hold centuries of history among their walls and corridors. Dating from the seventeenth century, Hacienda Temozón has been artfully adapted to a dramatic, luxurious resort by The Plan Group Hotels in the Yucatán. The overall effect is of a comfortable, old-world hacienda with modern aspirations. Originally built as a cattle estate, Temozón, which means "whirlwind" in Maya, was converted to the cultivation of henequén in the mid-nineteenth century. At the height of its production, the hacienda employed 640 workers. Today, the impressive property offers twenty-eight suites with private plunge pools and gardens and a variety of

intriguing color-drenched spaces—courtyards, portals, salons, a private chapel, and an underground cenote for swimming. President Ernesto Zedillo of Mexico and President Bill Clinton of the United States have even dined together in the hotel's open-air restaurant.

The past is very near the surface at Temozón: A long line of stone-carved serpent *canales*, or water spouts, extend from the deep-red wall of the hacienda's grand entrance. Once used for the field's irrigation system, they now spew forth water for decorative impact. Hidden behind the *casa de máquinas*, or machine house, is an open field originally used for drying henequén fibers. Today, *secaderos*, or metal drying racks, stand in stark symmetry, surrounded by a jogging path that winds through trees and around the old towering chimney.

Left: Hacienda Temozón's pool is a magnificent stretch of blue, topped off with stark stone columns.

Left, top: A natural underground well, or cenote, beckons the adventurous for a cool swim.

Above: The graceful, arched portal of Temozón's newly restored guest rooms are brightened in traditional colors.

HACIENDA SANTA ROSA Another innovative hacienda restoration by The Plan Group that succeeds in mixing twentieth-century comforts into seventeenth-century spaces is Hacienda Santa Rosa. Located near biosphere reserves and coastal sanctuaries for pink flamingos, the estate's brightly painted facade—in red, yellow, and blue—reveals its bold approach to design. Like Temozón, the pools here border on their own art form. Interiors display refined elements of Mexican design, and European-style furnishings are at home throughout the elegantly appointed rooms.

HACIENDA KATANCHEL Offering visitors a taste of Yucatán's native flora and fauna is Hacienda Katanchel, nestled on 740 acres east of Yucatán's charming colonial capital, Mérida. Abandoned for some thirty-five years, the sixteenth-century cattle estate was restored as an eco-friendly resort in 1997. During restoration, thirty-three workers' quarters were discovered in near ruin, hidden in the jungle's overgrowth. Reinvented as individual guest pavilions, they now feature private gardens, soaking pools, and stylish interiors that blend local crafts with contemporary pieces, including an engaging four-poster bed that is in itself a modern piece of metal sculpture. By contrast, locally woven henequén hammocks are strung inside and out, making mere relaxing something of an art form. Interiors in the main hacienda building are a mix of family antiques, furnishings borrowed from Europe's past, and hearty mineral specimens.

Opposite: Hacienda Katanchel's front porch reveals original stenciled walls, inviting hammocks and antique wicker furniture.

Above: Hacienda de los Santos is a tranquil oasis located in the heart of the colonial silver-mining town of Alamos, Sonora.

The estate is rich with spectacular birdwatching, and Mayan ruins are scattered throughout the grounds. Katanchel's eco-conscious owners have made protecting the natural environment a high priority. Like other haciendas in the region, the estate flourished during the time of *oro verde*, or green gold, when land was cleared and dedicated to the cultivation of henequén. A reforestation project is now underway to replenish the hardwood and fruit trees that almost disappeared during that period. Only biodegradable substances, including a nontoxic insecticide, are used in cleaning and washing. Additionally, turn-of-the-century windmills work sixteen wells, with water recycled into the land for irrigation.

HACIENDA DE LOS SANTOS Hacienda de los Santos is a luxurious resort nestled amidst the colonial silver-mining town of Alamos, Sonora. In addition to lush grounds covering five acres, the 60,000-square-foot restored hacienda boasts an impressive collection of colonial religious art, three tranquil swimming pools, spa services, a 6,000-bottle wine cellar, billiard room, and an authentic 1800s cantina relocated from Cuernavaca, Mexico.

Opposite: The sprawling Copper Canyon Riverside Lodge is a block-long hacienda restored to its former splendor by owner Skip McWilliams in Batopilas, Chihuahua.

Right: The Copper Canyon Riverside Lodge features a newly restored tiled dome.

COPPER CANYON RIVERSIDE LODGE In northern Mexico, a restored nineteenth-century hacienda has become the jewel of a former silver boomtown. Hidden at the bottom of a deep gorge in the heart of the Sierra, the Copper Canyon Riverside Lodge is a luxurious oasis in a vast wilderness. Arriving in the once-prosperous mining village of Batopilas, home to the world's richest silver mine in the 1880s, one is transported into an era of splendor. The rambling block-long ex-hacienda, once home to the town's richest merchants, is a mix of adobe, hand-hewn beams, and Victorian antiques. Tarahumara Indians were employed to set up a tile-making factory on site, and eighteen-foot logs were transported via footpath from the cliff-side mountains. Its many courtyards, shaded with bamboo and bougainvillea, lead to parlors with magnificent ceiling murals, pianos, and chandeliers.

Opposite: Hotel Hacienda Chichén lies among the strikingly picturesque Mayan ruins of Chichén-Itzá.

Above: This collonade is part of the Temple of the Warriors, Chichén Itzá, Yucatán.

Visitors are surrounded by lush Tarahumara country, ideal for birding or eco-adventures; endless trails lead to spectacular waterfalls, remote caves, hot springs, and the lost cathedral of Satevo. For the true hacienda enthusiast, hikes can be made to the San Miguel hacienda, the deserted Gothic adobe home of American Alexander Sheperd, who came to oversee the mining operations in the late-nineteenth century.

HOTEL HACIENDA CHICHÉN Built in the sixteenth century, Hotel Hacienda Chichén is resplendent with lush gardens, a charming chapel, and tranquil patios. The hacienda lies among the strikingly picturesque ruins of Chichén-Itzá. In 1923, the estate became the Carnegie Institute's Mayan expedition headquarters, and additional cottages were built to house archaeologists working on the nearby ruins.

HACIENDA DE SAN ANTONIO Nestled in the shadow of two volcanoes, Hacienda de San Antonio, a former coffee hacienda, has survived both a revolution and a volcanic eruption. Something of a miracle, the nineteenth-century hacienda has persevered to become a newly restored executive retreat in Colima. Surrounded by a dramatic volcanic-rock aqueduct—built to water the estate's coffee and sugarcane fields—the property's newest additions include a fifty-foot swimming pool, outdoor dining area, and private amphitheater.

HACIENDA SAN ANTONIO CHALANTÉ Taking the bed-and-breakfast approach one step further, Hacienda San Antonio Chalanté offers horse lovers an intimate hacienda experience with the combination of bed, breakfast, and stable. Located in the Yucatán south of the colonial town of Izamal, this sixteenth-century estate boasts two chapels built in the 1500s—one mysteriously never completed—and a wealth of bridle paths leading to Mayan ruins and hidden underground wells. Owners Diane Dutton and Ken Hardin restored the magnificent property several years ago and added an impressive stable of horses, allowing visitors a horseback view of the region's riches.

THE HACIENDA INFLUENCE

THE HACIENDA INFLUENCE HAS BEEN IN THE UNITED STATES FROM THE EARLIEST DAYS OF THE SEVENTEENTH CENTURY WHEN MEXICO BEGAN TO COLONIZE THE SOUTHWEST. IN THOSE EARLY DAYS, THE ARCHITECTURAL STYLES AND ELEMENTS THAT APPEARED IN present-day Arizona, New Mexico, and Texas were pared-down hacienda designs; however, many of these same characteristics have prevailed today with great popularity. Recent interpretations have also served to bridge the gap between primitive and progressive.

Grand in scale but not overdesigned, hacienda-influenced homes integrate the soulful character of Mexican antiques and architectural elements within contemporary contexts. The imagery associated with the hacienda has in itself come to be symbolic of something more. Designers and homeowners have found inspiration in the spirit of Mexico's great country estates and have built character into new residences and offices with the hacienda's hearty handcrafted elements. In Miami, Florida's chic, South Beach, the headquarters for EMI Records/Latin created innovative interiors with Mexican colonial doors, shutters, and furnishings, adding a handsome rich flavor to the *saltillo*-tile halls and high-tech screening rooms.

Not far from the Mexican border in West Texas, the Cibola Creek Ranch Resort is an intriguing adaptation to a historic adobe fortress completed by San Antonio architect Chris Carson. Within a rustic austere setting, Carson created a harmonious mix between the original adobe brick structure that included two defensive towers at opposite corners, traditional hacienda architectural details, and Mexican furnishings. Carson has also designed a contemporary stone hacienda-style home in the Texas Hill Country.

Overlooking the Pacific, Villa de Cumbre in California was designed in the hacienda style by architect Douglas W. Burdge.

PACIFIC PALISADES CALIFORNIA

On the West Coast, architect Douglas W. Burdge and designer Sarah Bartlett have incorporated Mexican design elements into hacienda-style homes throughout Cabo San Lucas, Baja California, and southern California. Most recently, Burdge designed a custom home in Pacific Palisades for clients who wanted to create a two-story Mexican-influenced home on their ocean-view property. From the early design stage of their collaborative efforts, they planned to incorporate Mexican building materials and custom accents into the project, including carved cantera stone for columns, entrances, quatrefoil windows, parapet trims, fireplace surrounds, flooring, and even the pool coping. Hand-painted glazed clay tiles were used on all bathroom surfaces, stair risers, and custom murals for outdoor fountains. The kitchen features tiled walls that sweep upwards to eight feet, surrounding the enormous fireplace. Another notable detail is the foyer's impressive vaulted ceiling, built with Mexicalli brick. Door headers and ceiling *vigas* are hundred-year-old recycled beams from Mexico. Special wrought-iron lighting fixtures and artworks—selected by the homeowner on buying trips to Mexico—were worked into the design, allowing for properly fitted spaces in which to showcase them.

Opposite: A grand entrance features Mexican mesquite doors.

Below: This Sonoran desert home is nestled beneath the Santa Rita Mountains, Arizona.

SONORAN DESERT ARIZONA

In the midst of the enchanting Sonoran landscape in southeastern Arizona, a vacation country estate recalls the idyllic locations of the grand haciendas nestled in the shadows of Mexico's Sierra Madre. Its pale yellow facade makes a pleasing profile nestled beneath the Santa Rita Mountains. The impressive walled compound was designed to accommodate massive mesquite entrance doors found in Mexico. Adding colonial charm throughout the home, stone surrounds decorate doors and windows, echoing the fine craftsmanship of Guadalajara's stonecutters.

The owners are avid collectors of contemporary art, and their collection of abstract paintings infuses a modern flair to their rooms appointed with antiques from Asia, Mexico, and Europe. The kitchen's roots are firmly planted in the Arizona desert, as the mesquite cabinets are made from local mesquite, renowned for its tremendous strength and durability. The wood's warm reddish-brown tones and beautiful grain make it an ideal wood for creating an impressive statement.

SAN ANTONIO TEXAS

Stone in many forms is the most dominant theme connecting the many courtyards of antique dealer and collector Fred Pottinger's hacienda-style compound in San Antonio. From stone walls, fountains, and patios to decorative carved-stone virgins, his home and gallery complex is a fascinating study in textures. For over thirty years, Pottinger has showcased the best of his world travels in this secluded arena. At its heart lies his antique gallery, Horse of a Different Color.

Finding inspiration in the traditional hacienda's layout of combining living and working spaces together in the one-walled compound, Pottinger purchased two bungalow properties in the '70s. Starting with two homes and two garages, Pottinger continued to expand, building a large open barn-like showroom, complete with a long portal. Inside and out, Pottinger's talent for elegantly mixing old and new is evident.

His passion for Mexico, however, is most apparent in his own home, where intriguing objects are scattered throughout. Candles heighten the sense of mystery and intrigue surrounding his eclectic collections. An ideal spot for cocktails, the sitting room opposite the

Opposite: A thick-slab mesquite carpenter's bench is the perch for a pair of lions that once sat atop gates of a Mexican hacienda.

Right: Stone spheres and an iron-cactus sculpture add interest to Fred Pottinger's central courtyard.

dining table is an intimate area surrounded by an impressive display of *santos*, jewelry, and silver and gold chalices from Europe and Latin America. Another favorite sitting area is the main salon, which is anchored by a grand piano and surrounded with grand-scale mirrors and charming paintings of Mexican colonial towns.

HACIENDA RESTORATIONS

MEXICO'S RICH ARCHITECTURAL LEGACY INCLUDES BOTH PRE-HISPANIC STRUCTURES AS WELL AS THE RICHNESS OF COLONIAL CHURCHES AND HACIENDAS. FROM PALACES IN MEXICO CITY TO BAROQUE CHAPELS ON REMOTE HACIENDAS, MEXICO'S WEALTH OF historical treasures, many in near ruin, continue to inspire awe. Mexico's 1920 census documented over 8,245 haciendas. Thousands still exist, which make up a vast but highly threatened cultural heritage.

The preservation of Mexico's colonial architecture has gained widespread importance in recent years. This restoration movement is focused on rediscovering Mexico's traditional building techniques and the architectural elements that impart soul to a structure. Age-old methods are being well utilized in the restoration of Mexico's haciendas as well as in new home construction throughout the United States.

The efforts of a pioneering group of architects, designers, artists, and preservationists have stimulated interest in Mexican design and created myriad benefits for the people and landscape of Mexico's surrounding communities. As village residents are becoming more involved with the preservation and maintenance of their rich artistic patrimony — including buildings, murals, furniture, and paintings — traditional restoration methods are shared and passed on to future generations.

Mistreated by time but touched by the grace of sound craftsmanship, the haciendas and colonial buildings deserve our attention for their complete authenticity and even a certain sensuous appeal. The structures and the elements that surround them show that there are many lessons to be learned from the homes that belong to a previous age. Today, the restoration of haciendas creates not only revived living

The chapel dome of Hacienda San José del Progreso was restored courtesy The Rodolfo Morales Cultural Foundation.

spaces or tourist venues but often breathes new life into the communities they inhabit. The Yucatán's high concentration of haciendas has attracted numerous restoration projects by innovative individuals as well as organizations, including The Plan Group Hotels, which has been instrumental in adapting key hacienda properties into luxury hotels.

Previous pages: Hacienda San José del Progreso's dramatic arches hold centuries of history.

Opposite and right: The restored Ex-Convento of Santo Domingo de Guzman dates from 1555 and was completed in the seventeenth century. With the assistance of The Rodolfo Morales Cultural Foundation, restoration began in 1995. In addition to rescuing the chapel, halls, and floors, a number of abandoned objects were found, including furniture, colonial paintings, and religious objects. Today, these treasures are on display in their restored condition in the second-floor museum.

Francisco Toledo and Rodolfo Morales are two renowned artists who have heralded the importance of rescuing and preserving Mexico's cultural heritage. Their impressive contributions and projects in their native Oaxaca are many. Their efforts include the restoration of numerous churches, convents, colonial buildings, and haciendas, inspiring an exciting quest for increased knowledge of architecture, interiors, and furnishings from the colonial period.

Through the generosity of painter Rodolfo Morales, The Rodolfo Morales Cultural Foundation was established in 1990. Its goals are the rescue and preservation of colonial architecture, popular arts and traditions, and the ecology of the state of Oaxaca. In Ocotlán, its outreach has contributed to the creation of restoration workshops, computer labs, libraries, and an open-air theater in Morales's native community. Additionally, efforts extend to Oaxaca's natural patrimony as well. Hundreds of purple-blooming *jacaranda* trees have been planted to enhance a seven-kilometer stretch of highway from San Martin Tilcajeteto to Ocotlán. Five thousand *copal* trees were also planted to allow village artisans a source of wood to carve their *alebrijes*, or carved animals. To date, the foundation counts over ten restoration projects to its credit, including the impressive sixteenth-century Ex-Convento of Santo Domingo de Guzmán in Ocotlán and the chapel at Hacienda San José del Progreso.

Working with The Rodolfo Morales Cultural Foundation, architects Esteban San Juan Maldonado and Eugen Logan Wagner have led many projects, including haciendas that are within *ejidos*, or community-owned properties. Working together with local residents, they have devised plans that involve the community in the adaptive reuse and restoration of their historical buildings, allowing them to benefit from new uses that bring tourism and employment. Fomento Social Banamex, under the direction of Fernando Peón, is seeking ways to fund the community self-help projects in rural areas. Several villages with haciendas in their midst are benefiting with grants to restore haciendas for community benefit. Two outstanding projects are Hacienda Cetelac in Yucatán and Hacienda Xaaga in Oaxaca.

Hacienda Xaaga represents over six centuries of history with its sequence of buildings that have evolved from the pre-Columbian era to the Revolution. Built by the Zapotecs as a palace for a ruling elite before the Spanish arrived, the Zapotecs transformed it into the Spanish equivalent of a hacienda in the early colonial period. Centered around a cruciform Zapotec tomb replete with the nearby Mitla-style *grecas*, or stone mosaic friezes, Xaaga evolved into a sprawling wheat and cattle hacienda. At present, plans for Xaaga include converting the ejido property into a combined-use new hacienda—a museum and a bed and breakfast.

Over the last twenty years, Francisco Toledo has been an untiring promoter of the cultural values of his native state. In addition to founding the Museo de Arte Contemporaneo de Oaxaca (MACO) and the Instituto de Artes Gráficas de Oaxaca (IAGO), Toledo has established the Patronato Por-Defensa y Conservación del Patrimonio Cultural y Natural del

Estado de Oaxaca (PROOAX) and numerous libraries and photography centers housed in restored colonial buildings.

Most recently Toledo has restored and transformed the former Etla Valley's local power plant into a paper mill that has revived the tradition of handmade quality natural fiber papermaking. In pre-Hispanic times, Oaxaca was a prominent paper capital producing codices paper. In addition to carrying on this artful craft, Taller Arte Papel Oaxaca provides local artists with a much-needed source for specialized paper materials.

The preservation movement has brought renewed momentum to the teaching of the arts of construction to local youths. Whether masonry, bricklaying, plastering, ironwork,

An old electric plant in the Oaxaca Valley has been restored and transformed into the Taller Arte Papel Oaxaca, *a new workshop producing traditional handmade fiber papers. Natural fibers, including* henequén, ixtle, *and cotton are used along with* baba de nopal, *or cactus juice, in the age-old papermaking process. Alberto Valenzuela Hernández is shown here with the moveable drying rack that holds the finished paper product.*

furniture, or painting restoration, mentors enable communities to form a connection to their own rich artistic patrimony.

To further promote the traditional building methods and adaptive reuse of haciendas and historic architecture in Mexico, special architectural programs under the umbrella of Studio Mexico have been founded by Professor Eugen Logan Wagner at the University of Texas and The College of Santa Fe.

The in-depth studies of these complex properties continue to reveal fascinating historical details relating to the hacienda's economic function on the local and national level, its adaptive roles during the colonial era and independence movement, and even hacienda family traditions—from recipes to celebrations. Consequently, the attention surrounding the hacienda movement also contributes to preserving vibrant and valuable history, bringing recognition to this rich dimension for future generations.

TRADITIONAL TECHNIQUES

Shaped in part by differing climates and topography, regional distinctions are found in many elements: adobe, *tapial*, or rammed earth, carved stone, coral stone, wood, thatching, and stucco using *baba de nopal*, or cactus juice. Decorative details also include *bóvedas*, or vaulted ceilings; forged iron work; talavera tile; *rajueleado*, a pre-Hispanic masonry-chinking technique; *alfarjes*, intricate Moorish wooden ceilings; and *tecalli*, a translucent onyx used for windows that has its roots in the pre-Hispanic era. Many of these techniques were brought over by the Spanish, who gained the knowledge from the Moors. Ironically, the craftsmanship in these regions has almost disappeared; however, in Mexico the knowledge has survived and continues to be passed on to future generations.

STONE The tradition of stone carving for both structural building elements as well as ornamentation are in high demand for door and window surrounds, arcades, columns with elaborate Corinthian-style capitals, fountains, statuary, and fireplaces. Stone colors range from green hues in Oaxaca to pink in Guanajuato to orange and brown tones in Zácatecas. The Yucatán boasts a speckled deep-orange *cantera* from Ticul. Volcanic stones like the maroon-colored *xitle* and the extremely hard black *recinto* are prevalent in the vicinity of Mexico City.

RAJUELEADO Although its purpose since pre-Hispanic times was to reinforce the grout between the brick or stone courses, present-day architects have prescinded from using stucco to cover the walls; rather, they exhibit the aesthetic qualities afforded by the patterns created with diverse chinking materials: stone pebbles, brick pieces, or even pottery shards are quite the norm. The addition of decomposed brick or old shards to mortar (stucco) increases its weather resistance. One unique wall construction is found at the former sugar estate, Hacienda San Gabriel de las Palmas in Morelos, which features large, ceramic, cone-shaped vessels once used to form the unrefined sugar cones called *piloncillos*.

ADOBE Sun-dried mud bricks as a building material have been used in many cultures throughout the world and have seen a popular renewal of interest in recent years in both grand-scale homes and humble abodes.

TAPIAL, **OR RAMMED EARTH** This technique of packing earth into forms for building is enjoying a resurgence in the United States and Australia because it holds great potential for new construction, allowing one to achieve the massive walls for niches, deep windows, and *bancos*, or built-in benches. It also allows for the concealment of plumbing, electrical, and cable lines.

BÓVEDAS, **OR VAULTS** This traditional masonry vaulting technique was brought to Mexico by the Spanish. Vaults can be constructed of low-fired brick, carved-stone ashlars, or even unfired adobe brick. Types of vaults include *bóveda de cañon* (barrel vault), *bóveda de arista* (groined vault), *bóveda media naranja* (hemispheric vault), and *bóveda eliptica* (elyptic vault). With these traditional methods passed down through the generations, family teams of bóvederos are centered around the town of Lagos de Moreno in Jalisco, Mexico.

PLASTERS AND STUCCOES Depending on the finished texture desired, a vast array of traditional methods offer beautiful and multiple textural effects. Because it is more porous than modern Portland cement, lime mortar allows the masonry walls to "breathe" and lets trapped moisture evaporate, thus preventing coving and possible structural damage to the walls. Because of its extreme hardness, Portland cement mortar should be avoided because it weathers at a much slower rate than the masonry units in stone, brick, or adobe; it is bonding, creating an unsightly and bizarre grid of cement mortar joints, jutting from the wall.

Evidence of lime-burning in prehistoric times was found when a lime kiln dating from about 2450 BC was excavated at Khafe, Mesopotamia. The Maya were using lime mortar as early as AD 300, and most of the Yucatán and Palenque is built with lime mortar and *sascaab*, another limestone found in the Yucatán region.

Limestone mortar is created through the following steps:

BURNING—Limestone is traditionally burned in pits or kilns (900 degrees centigrade) to create *cal viva*, or quicklime.

SLAKING, OR HYDRATION—The quicklime mixture is mixed with water and produces a thermal reaction that is very hot. Quicklime and water combined create slaked lime.

REVERSION, OR HARDENING—Mixing the slaked lime with water and sand creates mortar.

Plaster is similar to lime mortar, but instead of limestone, the stone that is burned is calcium sulfate. Requiring less heat, plaster is used for interiors and ornamental work. Egg yolks, marble dust, colored clays, and *baba de nopal*, or nopal cactus juice, are a few of the ingredients often used to create a variety of finishes. The viscosity of baba de nopal provides a resiliency that helps prevent cracking.

Enlucido plaster is accomplished by rubbing the surface with a *frates*, or mushroom-shaped wooden trowel. In pre-Hispanic Mexico, a stone polisher was utilized. Other plasters include *rústico* (rustic), *púlido* (polished), *bruñidos* (burnished), and *hidráulico* (hydraulic).

Pintura de cal, or lime-based wash, includes pigmentation and is used to paint walls. *Tlapalerias*, or colonial-era hardware stores of Mexico, still offer pintura de cal.

The Morelia home of Ed Holler and Sam Saunders features a restored building that once housed the colonial estate's horse carriages. Today, the space is used as an entertainment salon and boasts a statue from an old Mexican cinema.

RESOURCES

WE INVITE YOU TO VISIT OUR GALLERY, JOE P. CARR DESIGN, FOR MEXICAN COLONIAL ANTIQUES AND HACIENDA ARCHITECTURAL ELEMENTS, INCLUDING OLD DOORS, WROUGHT-IRON WINDOW GRILLES, CEILING BEAMS AND FLOORING. IN ADDITION TO ANTIQUE TRUNKS, TABLES AND BENCHES, WE ALSO OFFER A COLLECTION OF CUSTOM HACIENDA TABLES BY JOE CARR, FEATURING RECLAIMED MEXICAN HARDWOODS. DECORATIVE ACCENTS INCLUDE ANTIQUE CERAMICS, SANTOS, CROSSES, OLD STONE ELEMENTS AND HACIENDA PHOTOGRAPHS.

Please visit our web site at www.mexicanstyle.com for Mexican design news.

www.mexicanstyle.com

Authors' Mailing Address:
JOE P. CARR &
KAREN WITYNSKI
3267 Bee Caves Rd. # 107 - 181
Austin, TX 78746
512.370.9663
512.328.2966 fax

Authors' Gallery:
JOE P. CARR DESIGN
3601 Bee Caves Road
at Barton Springs Nursery
Austin, TX 78746
512.327.8284

KAREN WITYNSKI
ARCHITECTURAL &
INTERIOR PHOTOGRAPHY
512.370.9663
512.328.2966 fax

Top: Authors Joe P. Carr and Karen Witynski.

Middle: Traditional Yucatán door.

Ceramic tamalero pots rest atop a " Mexican Ranch Table" by Joe Carr.

A Spanish-style table designed by Joe Carr anchors the dramatic comedor (dining room) at Hacienda Petac, Yucatán, Mexico.

U.S. GALLERIES

ANTIGUA DE MEXICO
7037 N. Oracle Road
Tucson, AZ 85704
520.742.7114

ARTES DE MEXICO
1000 Chestnut Street
Burbank, CA 91506
818.753.4559

CASA LOCA
1130 N. Milwaukee
Chicago, IL 60622
773.278.2972

CIERRA INTERIORS
5502 Burnet Road
Austin, TX 78756
512.454.8603

CIERRA INTERIORS
2920 N. Henderson Avenue
Dallas, TX 75206
214.887.8772

CIERRA INTERIORS
2418 W. Alabama
Houston, TX 77098
713.942.9001

CIERRA INTERIORS
9985 IH-10 West
San Antonio, TX 78230
210.877.1700

CITA RESORT INTERIORS
129 N. Alister
Port Aransas, TX 78373
361.749.2711
361.749.2714 fax

CLAIBORNE GALLERY
418 Cerrillos Road
Santa Fe, NM 87501
505.982.8019

ELEGANTE
500 N. Lamar
Austin, TX 78703
512.236.0068

EL VIDA
1516 Beech Street
McAllen, TX 78502
956.686.6086

FOUR WINDS GALLERY
5512 Walnut Street
Pittsburgh, PA 15232
412.683.2895

GALERIA SAN YSIDRO
801 Texas Avenue
El Paso, TX 79917
915.544.4444

GLORIA LIST ART & ANTIQUES
418 Cerrillos Road
Santa Fe, NM 87501
505.982.5622

HOLLER & SAUNDERS
By Appointment Only
Nogales, AZ 85628
520.287.5153

HORSE OF A DIFFERENT COLOR
140 W. Sunset
San Antonio, TX 79917
210.824.9762

JOSHUA BAER & CO.
925 Old Santa Fe Trail
Santa Fe, NM 87501
505.988.8944

MI CASA GALLERY
1700-A S. Congress
Austin, TX 78704
512.707.9797

MIKE HASKELL ANTIQUES
539 San Ysidro Road
Santa Barbara, CA 93108
805.565.1121

NUEVO SANTANDER GALLERY
717 N. Main Street
McAllen, TX 78501
956.618.4959

OSCAR'S ANTIQUES
1002 Guadalupe
Laredo, TX 78040
956.723.0765

PACHAMAMA
223 Canyon Road
Santa Fe, NM 87501
505.983.4020

PETER GRAU GALLERY
142 S. Cedros Avenue
Solana Beach, CA 92075
858.259.0353

THE SPANISH CROSS
2629 E. Broadway Boulevard
Tucson, AZ 85716
520.322.5383

TEXTURE ANTIQUES
3601 Bee Caves Road
at Barton Springs Nursery
Austin, TX 78746
512.327.8284

TIERRA DULCE
5403 S. Rice, #D
Houston, TX 77081
713.838.7770

WILSON CLEMENTS
P.O. Box 797
Comfort, TX 78013
830.995.5039

YUCATÁN BAMBOO, INC.
5 Woods Edge Lane
Houston, TX 77024
713.278.7344 in U.S.
866.514.3986 toll-free
997.971.02.45 in Mexico

ZÓCALO FINE FOLK ART & FURNITURE
321 W. 19th Street
Houston, TX 77008
713.869.1501

MEXICO GALLERIES

THE RODOLFO MORALES CULTURAL
FOUNDATION
Murgula #105, Col. Centro
Oaxaca, Oaxaca 68000

ARCHITECTS

LOGAN WAGNER
1416 Alameda Drive
Austin, TX 78704
512.441.9729

LABEN WINGERT
P.O. Box 2045
Santa Fe, NM 87501
505.983.7200

BURDGE & ASSOCIATES
Douglas W. Burdge
21235 Pacific Coast Highway
Malibu, CA 90265
310.456.5905

FORD, POWELL AND CARSON
1138 E. Commerce Street
San Antonio, TX 78205
210.226.1246

MUSEUMS

HACIENDA OCHIL
Henequén Museum & Restaurant
Km 175 Carr. Mérida-Uxmal
999.993.99.77
999.023.80.89

HACIENDA YAXCOPOIL
MUSEUM & PARADOR
Km 186, Fed. Hwy 261 Mérida-Uxmal
999.927.26.06
www.yaxcopoil.com

MUSEO DE MUEBLES
Hacienda El Lencero
Veracruz, Mexico

MARTINEZ HACIENDA
Ranchitos Road (RD 240)
Taos, NM 87571
505.758.1000

THE MEXICAN MUSEUM
Fort Mason Center
Laguna & Marina Boulevards
San Francisco, CA 94123
415.441.0445

MEXIC-ARTE MUSEUM
419 Congress Avenue
Austin, TX 78768
512.480.9373

MEXICAN FINE ARTS CENTER MUSEUM
1852 W. 19th Street
Chicago, IL 60608
312.738.1503

SAN ANTONIO MUSEUM OF ART
200 W. Jones
San Antonio, TX 78125
210.978.8116

Colonial trunk at Texture Antiques.

"Hacienda Round Table" by Joe Carr.

TRAVEL

We have compiled this select listing of colonial haciendas, hotels, restaurants and museums from our years of traveling throughout Mexico. Additional listings can be found on our web site at **www.mexicanstyle.com**.

HACIENDA HOTELS

THE HACIENDAS
The Luxury Collection
Starwood Hotels &
Resorts Worldwide Inc.
Owners: Grupo Plan

HACIENDA SAN JOSÉ CHOLUL, Yucatán
HACIENDA SANTA ROSA, Yucatán
HACIENDA TEMOZÓN, Yucatán
HACIENDA UAYAMÓN, Campeche

Managed by Starwood Hotels &
Resorts:
999.923.80.89
999.923.79.63 fax
800.325.3589 toll-free in U.S.
800.909.4800 toll-free in Mexico
52.1.555.242.5650 outside Mexico
www.luxurycollection.com

HACIENDA SAN ANTONIO
Municipio Tixkokob, Yucatán
999.910.61.44
www.haciendasanantonio.com.mx

HACIENDA TEYA
Hotel—Restaurant—Events
Km 12.5, Carr. Mérida
Cancún, Yucatán
999.988.08.01

HACIENDA XCANATÚN
Km 12, Carr. Mérida-Progreso
Mérida, Yucatán
999.941.02.13
888.883.3633 toll-free
www.xcanatun.com

HOTEL HACIENDA CHICHÉN
at Chichén Itzá Archeological Site
Chichén Itzá, Yucatán
985.851.00.45
800.624.8451 in U.S.
www.yucatantravel.com

HACIENDA CHALANTÉ
Sudzal, Yucatán
999.954.02.87

HACIENDA KATANCHEL
Km 26, Highway 180
Tixkokob, Yucatán
888.882.9740 toll-free in U.S.
999.923.40.20

HACIENDA DE CORTES
Plaza Kennedy 9
Cuernavaca, Morelos
73.15.88.44

HACIENDA DE SAN ANTONIO
Comala, Col. Mexico
A.P. 2-1676 Suc. Manuel Alvarez
Colima, Colima 28000
331.342.29

HACIENDA DE LOS SANTOS
Calle Molina #8
Alamos, Sonora
642.80222

HACIENDA SAN MIGUEL REGLA
Carr. Mexico-Pachuca
San Miguel Regla, Hidalgo
213.462.6391 in U.S.
779.20102 in Mexico

CASA DE ESPIRITUS
Ex-Hacienda La Trinidad
Marfil, Guanajuato
408.423.0181 in U.S.
473.31013 in Mexico

BEYOND THE HACIENDA

ALBERTO'S CONTINENTAL
PATIO RESTAURANT
Calle 64, #482
Mérida, Yucatán
999.928.53.67

LA MISIÓN DE FRAY DIEGO
Calle 61, #524, Col. Centro
Mérida, Yucatán
999.924.11.11
www.lamisiondefraydiego.com

HOTEL CASA DEL BALAM
Calle 60, #488
Mérida, Yucatán
800.624.8451 toll-free in U.S.
999.924.21.50

CAMINO REAL HOTEL
Ex-Convento Santa Catalina
Calle Cinco de Mayo 300
Oaxaca, Oaxaca
951.60611

LA OLLA CAFE
Reforma 402, Centro
Oaxaca, Oaxaca
951.66668

LAS BUGAMBILIAS HOTEL
Reforma 402, Centro
Oaxaca, Oaxaca
951.61165

BOOKS

A few of our favorite books from
Mexico are listed below.

Bartlett, Paul Alexander.
*The Haciendas of Mexico: An Artist's
Record.* Boulder: University Press of
Colorado, 1990.

Bishop, William Henry.
Old Mexico and Her Lost Provinces.
New York: Harper & Brothers, 1889.

Colle, Marie Pierre.
Casa Poblana. Monterrey, Mexico:
Museo de Monterrey, 1993.

Garcini, Ricardo Rendón.
Haciendas de Mexico. Mexico City:
Fomento Cultural Banamex, A.C., 1994.

—*Vida Cotidiana en Las Haciendas de
Mexico.* Mexico City: Fomento Cultural
Banamex, A.C., 1997.

Garrison, G. Richard, and George
Rustay. *Early Mexican Houses.*
Stamford, CT: Architectural Book
Publishing Co., 1930; 1990.

Yampolsky, Mariana.
La Casa Que Canta.
Mexico City: SEP, 1982.

PHOTOGRAPHIC CREDITS

Photographs are by © W. Scott Mitchell unless otherwise noted below.

Numbers indicate pages.

Key: T —Top Row
          M —Middle
          B —Bottom
          L —Left
          C —Center
          R —Right

Alva, Luis Guerrero, *Las Haciendas de Hidalgo*: xix

Ballheim, Ray: 45

Carr, Joe P.: 14T, 15TL, 15ML, 46, 54, 114

Chacel, Jorge Contreras/Fomento Cultural Banamex, A.C.: 63
Hacienda San Pedro Ovando, Municipio de Acatzingo, Puebla

Gomez, Mario: 58

Kenny, Gill: 23, 136, 137

Lohman, Mark: 135

Spahn, James Ray: Cover, Contents, 41, 42, 43, 44, 47, 48C, 139, 154T

Snyder, Jeff: 130

Vertikoff, Alexander: 22, 34, 37, 38, 152, 153

Witynski, Karen: Copyright page, 13T, 14BL, 14BR, 18TL, 18BL, 18BR, 48L, 49, 55, 78, 81B, 100, 132, 138, 147BR, 154M, 154B, 155, 157, 158, 159, 160, 161

Yampolsky, Mariana: 27, 30, 32, 33

Illustrations by Julie Marshall: 67, 68, 69

Illustrations by Paul Alexander Bartlett: 29

We thank the following publications for their permission to reprint their photographs in our book:

Las Haciendas de Hidalgo,
Governor of the State Hidalgo, Lic. Manuel Angel Nuñez Soto;
Publication Director, Lic. Gustavo Torres Campos: 19, 31

Haciendas de Mexico, Fomento Cultural Banamex, A.C.,: 63

Illustration courtesy *Mexico and Her Lost Provinces:* 28

Haciendas of Mexico: An Artist's Record,
University Press of Colorado: 29

Copper Canyon Riverside Lodge: 131

Hacienda de Los Santos: 128

Hacienda Temozón: 125T

Colophon
The body text, set in Matrix, was designed by Zuzana Licko circa 1986. Chapter openings and subheads are set in Matrix Narrow and captions are set in Matrix Script.